WOMEN

IN THE

WORKFORCE

WOMEN IN THE WORKFORCE

HUMAN RESOURCE DEVELOPMENT STRATEGIES INTO THE NEXT CENTURY

Edited by
Sheena Briley

EDINBURGH: HMSO

HMSO Scotland, South Gyle Crescent
Edinburgh EH12 9EB

Applications for reproduction should be made to HMSO

British Library Cataloguing in Publication Data
A catalogue record for this book is available from the British Library

ISBN 0 11 495733 9

Cover illustration by Steve Earl

'When I came here I thought of myself as a Kenyan woman.
Now I think of myself as a woman.'
Joan Wena, Kenya

CONTENTS

Preface

This book brings together a collection of voices from professionals in the field of gender and human resource development, all of whom offer us their thoughts and ideas on women's position at work and in society today.

The views represented in this book are as wide-ranging as the diverse backgrounds of the contributors themselves. Leading professionals from industry and commerce, education and academia, human resource specialists, and experts from non-governmental-organisations have all come together here to reflect on the enormous changes taking place throughout society at the present time in regard to the changing roles of women and men.

Examining a variety of current issues – including the position of women in management, access to information, work and training, and the arenas of decision-making, politics and the law – we look at the position of women in urban and rural communities. We have also included contributions from women in startlingly different social and economic positions to our own in the UK, with a picture of women from the developing economy of Swaziland, and from a country in economic transition, Poland.

What is striking is that, although the contributors are writing from very different viewpoints and with contrasting experiences, what binds them together is a desire to make progress in equalising opportunities for women and men – as a fundamental aspect of human rights, and as a vital component of social and economic growth.

As we approach the end of the twentieth century, the key issues for women, it seems, are to do with access to information, enabling women to have, and to make, choices in their lives. Also included in this book are thoughts on how we can break down the barriers which inhibit women's freedom in making choices, and which, if we do not take action now, will continue to limit the freedom and choices of future generations.

Although a great deal has been achieved in the quest for an equal world, much remains to be done. This book serves as a useful reminder that it is women the world over who predominantly undertake work that is of low value, and it is women who are the very poorest people in society. I hope that some of the ideas presented here will give us an opportunity to reflect on the present situation, as well as suggesting ways to go forward. Now, after the United Nations Fourth World Conference on Women, we can all work towards, and look forward to, a future where choices for women and men will not be limited because of gender.

Sheena Briley, Director, TRAINING 2000

FOREWORD

In June 1995, TRAINING 2000, the charity which promotes training for women, teamed up with the British Council in Edinburgh to deliver a week-long international seminar, 'Women in the Workforce: Human Resource Development Strategies into the Next Century'.

The seminar focused on current issues in human-resource development in relation to gender, and attracted participants from all over the world who work in this field, in the public and private sectors and in non-governmental organisations.

It seemed to us that the information which had been presented there, by a range of experts in the field of women's training and development, ought to be disseminated to a wider audience, particularly in view of the fact that the seminar preceded the United Nations Fourth World Conference on Women, held in Beijing in September 1995. We are, therefore, delighted that this publication will enable others to access some of the information gathered there, and we view this book as a valuable resource.

Our aim is that this publication will make a useful contribution to the current discussion and debate around women's access to training and education, and will stimulate further innovative initiatives.

Tony Andrews, Director, British Council, Scotland
Barbara Kelly, Chairwoman, TRAINING 2000

◆

ACKNOWLEDGEMENTS

My thanks are due to all those who were able to accept our invitation to speak at the seminar, some of whose contributions are incorporated in this book.

I would like to thank the delegates from around the world who attended the seminar, whose own insights and contributions were most valuable. Special thanks must go to the very able chairwomen of the seminar, who brought their own specialist area of expertise to the proceedings. Thanks are also due to the staff of the British Council in Edinburgh, and particular thanks go to the then Director of the British Council in Scotland, Tony Andrews.

I am grateful to the Management Board of TRAINING 2000 for their work and encouragement in this project, in particular to Barbara Kelly CBE, Chairwoman of TRAINING 2000, and the TRAINING 2000 staff team of Louie Larkin, Andrea McHugh and Rosemary MacKinnon. Special thanks go to Elaine Henderson, who worked for us on this publication throughout the summer of 1995.

We received excellent sponsorship for the seminar, and we would like to thank the following for their support: the European Commission, Representation in Scotland; the City of Edinburgh District Council; Lothian Regional Council; Lothian and Edinburgh Enterprise Limited; and Scottish Enterprise.

Two important organisations sponsored this publication, namely Scottish Enterprise and Highlands and Islands Enterprise, and I would particularly like to thank Dennis Sim at Scottish

Enterprise and Ralph Palmer at Highlands and Islands Enterprise for their support from a very early stage of this project.

Finally, I would like to thank Alastair Holmes and Gillian Kerr of HMSO for their continued and much-appreciated support, advice and expertise.

Sheena Briley, Director, TRAINING 2000

Part 1

Current Issues in Women's Management Development

Chapter 1

◆

Current Issues in Women's Management Development and Training

Lex Gold

The Changing Nature of Work

Before tackling the issue of women's management development and training, it would seem sensible to explore a little the changed and changing nature of business and employment. This is not a politician's ploy to avoid the issue, but an attempt to tackle it within the context of what is happening in our labour market.

Work is changing. The future of the labour market is not going to be like the past. All the statistics show that working practices have been changing in a consistent direction over the last decade or so. 'Womb-to-tomb' employment – a lifetime spent with one employer – is becoming the exception rather than the rule, and several trends are emerging to produce that outcome. Part-time employment has increased by around a quarter over the last fifteen years, and it has been estimated that 45 per cent of all employees will be working part-time by the year 2003. There have also been similar patterns of increase in self-employment throughout the UK, an average of 11 per cent of workers now being self-employed. This means that, already, full-time per-manent employees make up under two-thirds of the workforce. The other third, around 10 million people, are employed on a part-time, temporary or self-employed basis, an increase of 1 million since 1986. In addition, there are the registered unemployed. These are striking changes to anyone used to the traditional full-time, 'job-for-life' culture. What has brought them about?

The first reason is fairly straightforward. People are not doing the same kinds of jobs any more. Throughout the 1980s there was a large change in the make-up of British industry, with the decline of many traditional areas – like heavy manufacturing – and an increase in others, particularly in the service sector. This has had implications for employment patterns. Different industries work in different ways. Relatively speaking, the industries that saw most decline in the 1980s went in for the traditional masculine, 'womb-to-tomb' pattern. A good example is mining, rather more than the newer service industries, where there are more women employed, generally on a part-time basis.

Some argue that, given the concentration of these new part-time jobs in the unappealingly-titled 'miscellaneous services' sector, it is likely that a significant number are relatively low-paid and low-status jobs. That may be so; but the growth of part-time work has also reflected supply-side pressure from women who do not want to work full-time because of family responsibilities. The majority of women working part-time appear to prefer this form of employment over full-time work. Indeed, an OECD study recently suggested that there were five times as many full-timers who wanted to be part-timers as there were part-timers who wanted to be full-timers.

It should not be forgotten that the potential workforce is actually larger now than it ever used to be, as more women have joined it. Therefore, employment itself has changed. This change in the make-up of the economy can account for most of the change in the 1980s. That people are, on aggregate, working at different jobs is significant enough; but, over the last few years, there has been evidence that, even within particular businesses, patterns of work are changing.

This first started becoming apparent in a survey of benefits packages which the Confederation of British Industry (CBI) conducted towards the end of 1992. When asked about the changes that they had seen in the last five years, 36 per cent of businesses said that they had seen more part-time working and 36 per cent said that they had seen a shortening of the length of service. The length of the average UK employee's history with their present employer was four years in 1990; but although this had risen in 1994, paradoxically, to five years, not too much should be read into these figures. In the past, individuals decided to move, and now they are perhaps less confident about doing so; and average current tenure in the UK is significantly shorter than in France and Germany. There are reasons to believe that the trend will be towards more changes in employment for each individual in the future. The business agenda over the next ten years will be dominated by the need to adapt to increasing global competition. In the future, therefore, commercial success will require:

- new approaches to attracting, retaining and motivating people;
- the development of flexible and flatter organisations with greater delegation of responsibility and authority;
- management styles which take account of the demands of a better-educated, more self-confident and independent workforce;
- fast, frequent and efficient communications between and with employees;
- greater emphasis on individuals, extending their responsibilities and building their commitment to the values and goals of the organisations; and

- reward strategies focused on the performances and needs of individuals.

The structures required to allow businesses to operate in this way will differ from sector to sector.

A Vision of the Future?

One image which has become familiar is that of smaller businesses run by smaller groups of people – smaller businesses which may well still be part of a very large concern, but with much greater freedom of decision-making. That may include more power to decide terms and conditions of employment, and power to take on part-time, temporary and subcontractor workers whose employment with the organisation may come and go. The core group of employees themselves may not be full-time nor expect to stay with their employer for life.

There may well be more employees working away from the office, supported by some of the new technologies now emerging from the telecommunications industry. Thus, we may be moving towards some 'virtual' employees working in 'virtual' offices. Certainly, the emerging technological changes carry even bigger organisational implications: paper-based bureaucracies are being replaced by electronic information transfer across departmental boundaries. Future competitive requirements to be first in the marketplace imply more horizontal transfer of information, using advanced technology, rather than the traditional vertical and hierarchical approach. Middle management grades whose role was to gather and analyse information are disappearing. Already there is less demarcation between manager and managed at all levels and a lessening both of status and of the power that comes simply from being privy to information. Given that women tend to be concentrated in lower management grades, it would appear unlikely that removing middle management and flattening the structure will be of any help in getting women to hold more than the current 2 per cent of senior positions. It may well just increase the competition.

Unsurprisingly, OECD data suggests that short tenure in employment correlates to poor training, and less of it. In the USA, 92 per cent of those who have been with their firm for under a year have received no formal training; although if they stay for fifteen years, that proportion still without formal training only falls to 75 per cent. The conclusions of the 1993 OECD employment outlook were that 'roughly, training increases with employment stability', and that there can be a link between enterprise skill training and tenure: 'too high a rate of labour turnover does not facilitate the development of workplace skills'. Rapid labour turnover, driven by corporate re-engineering, restructuring, downsizing, or 'industrial anorexia', also brings morale problems, which affect the longer-term motivation of individuals, and of course companies themselves. What employees hear is that they are the firm's most valuable assets.

This theme has been taken up by Robert Reich, President Clinton's Secretary of Labour. In *The Work of Nations: Preparing for Twenty-first Century Capitalism* he writes,

> There will be no national products or technologies, no national corporations, no national industries ... All that will remain rooted within national borders are the people that comprise a nation. Each nation's primary assets will be its citizens' skill and insights.

In Reich's view, all the world's workers are now part of an international labour market. It is the quality of the workforce in any part of the world which will determine the quality of the jobs which global businesses choose to locate there. High added-value jobs in research and development, in complex engineering functions, in strategic planning or corporate development, will be sited wherever skilled scientists, engineers, analysts and managers can be found. This is not a theoretical point, but has important practical consequences. It means that our foremost priority must be to educate and train our workforce, both present and future, so that we can have uniquely attractive, or at least competitive, skills and advantages to offer to the world. This requires that we draw on all available talent; the only discrimination should be on the basis of ability.

The Position of Women in the Workforce

In the UK in 1993, 71 per cent of women in the 16–59 age group were economically active, representing an increase of 16 per cent over the nine years since 1984. Of this increase, 40 per cent was in part-time working, and estimates suggest that between now and the end of the century there will be a further 750,000 jobs for women.

The 1993 Labour Force Survey discovered that 83 per cent of women working part-time did not want full-time work, while only 9 per cent would have preferred full-time work. (About 1 million men worked part-time, but only about a third of them were satisfied with part-time work.) In the UK in 1993, women made up about 49 per cent of the workforce, and in 1993 slightly more women than men received job-related training. In Scotland over this period, the position was reversed: about two-thirds of women's jobs in Scotland were concentrated in distribution, hotels and catering, repairs and other services. On pay, the record here is even poorer than in the rest of the UK, which is itself no paragon. The rest of Europe is also not much better.

Women are also under-represented at senior levels in the professions and in management: fewer than 10 per cent are managers, and their numbers dropped during the recession.

Progress has been made in helping to redress these imbalances; but it is slow, as there is no single panacea. Pressure needs to be maintained on a range of issues embracing equal pay, childcare (where the CBI has called for a national strategy) and universal nursery provision. There also needs to be a review of the benefit and tax system to ensure that working women are not penalised and to ensure that there are no barriers to entry and re-entry into the labour market.

In order to maintain and enhance the investment of employers and individuals in the development of those individuals employed, attention needs to be given to the level and quality of these jobs and to the opportunities for progression and development that should accompany them. This is in line with a broader need in the area of equal opportunities, highlighted in the CBI's equal-opportunities statement launched in September 1993 to extend the focus of positive action beyond recruitment to training, development and progression.

The results of the 1993 Labour Force Survey carry encouraging indicators. Slightly more women than men received training in the four weeks preceding the response date in the spring of 1993, and the training which they received was largely of a similar duration. The exception was for training of three years or more, where more men appeared to be involved. There is, unfortunately, no measure of training quality in this survey, but it suggests that opportunities for development do exist. Speculation might suggest that the reasons for women's scarcer representation in longer-term training programmes could include the prospect of career interruption due to family responsibilities. There is also some evidence that the training situation may improve in the competence environment of National Vocational Qualifications (NVQs) and Scottish Vocational Qualifications (SVQs), particularly through the accreditation of prior learning.

But if the prospects for training opportunities are more positive, those for progression demonstrate that there is still far to go. The report that Opportunity 2000 companies have seen some improvement in the prospects for progression for women is encouraging; but Labour Force Survey figures point to women being under-represented, both in the managerial or administrative and the professional grades. Clearly, many factors account for these differences, significant among them being the difficulties of balancing family and professional responsibilities, which force many women to interrupt their careers – including, perhaps, the lack of opportunity for more flexible working at these levels.

A number of complex factors are involved in the progress, or lack of it, that women make in the workplace, and many of them are cultural and represent values normally prescribed by men. In that context, it is foolish to view the workplace and its organisation as remarkably different from the society in which the work takes place. It is also too easy to blame the views that men have of women's roles. While there is undoubted truth in that charge, it is also, perhaps, the case that a number of women also subscribe to, or conspire with, these stereotypes. Culture takes time to change; it is not a rapid process. Although huge strides have been made in the recent past in the UK, it may take another generation before a complete breakthrough occurs. I appreciate that this is a rather gloomy view, and hope that it proves to be wrong, as indeed was my view in the late 1980s when claiming that the 'demographic time-bomb', which saw a considerable reduction in the numbers of younger people entering the workplace, would provide a huge boost to women's progress. In speeches, I used to ask women not to waste a great deal of energy on the moral issue of injustice and inequality in the workplace, not because this was acceptable but because it was more positive to seize the opportunity of the reduction in the number of school-leavers as a more pragmatic way of making progress. This approach was frustrated in part by the changes in the work-force described above, and also by the fairly deep recession which the UK, in common with much of Europe, then entered. Progress was made, however, because those who were promoting the cause of women in the workplace at that time, and since, helped to raise awareness of the issues. Women's training and development made big strides in the late 1980s by virtue of positive action. At that time, at the Manpower Services Commission in Scotland, we helped to promote courses on assertiveness for women, single-sex training and non-stereotypical training for young women. Coaching and mentoring have also been used to good effect.

The Way Forward
Looking ahead, my view is that we will not return quickly, if ever, to hierarchical structures in our companies. Flatter structures are likely to remain, and we will see increases in teamworking and empowerment. It is hoped that an enhanced emphasis on efficiency of performance will enable women to make progress within this future environment. But it has to be recognised, as suggested earlier, that a flatter structure is likely to lead to more, not less, competition for senior jobs. The UK government, too, is committed to raising the skills of the British workforce, and appears to accept the Robert Reich view of the future. The setting of national targets for education and training in 1991 was introduced to ensure that we in the UK competed with the best in the world in achieving educational and training competences. I tend, however, to share the concerns expressed by Alan Felstead, of the Centre for Labour Market Studies at the University of

Leicester, about the publicly-financed training from the Local Enterprise Companies and the Training and Enterprise Councils. He found an absence of financial incentives for support programmes which seek to open up training opportunities for women in non-traditional occupations. He also concluded that financial incentives work in the opposite direction, with positive outcomes being more likely to be achieved by placing individuals in sex-stereotypical occupations. Single-sex courses are more costly, and reliance on employer contributions makes it risky to challenge sexual prejudice. Felstead was also gloomy about initiatives to empower individuals, which he regarded as unlikely to break down occupational stereotypes. In Scotland, our Local Enterprise Companies are aware of the difficulties and attempt to tackle them; but the current government-funded courses are unlikely to lead to a major breakthrough.

In general, one can expect to see incremental progress in reducing inequality in our workplace. The best route appears to be that of bringing about a change in the way in which we view the contribution that men and women make in society more generally. Good progress has been made on this front, and we should not necessarily strive constantly to change matters by means of positive action initiatives. After almost ten years of working for change in this context, I have come to the view that an incremental and culture-change approach, to which positive action of course contributes, is most likely to bring about lasting change. Incremental change does not mean smaller steps; some could be quite large, if not even, in their development.

As a nation, the UK has experienced agrarian and industrial revolutions, and can now be said to be in the midst of an information revolution, in which there is, and will continue to be, a greater premium on brains, skill and dexterity than on brawn or muscle. This provides a comparative advantage to women. Could it be, therefore, that the British Council will host an international seminar in perhaps thirty or forty years' time to look at the problems faced by men in the workforce?

Chapter 2

◆

USING HUMAN RESOURCE DEVELOPMENT TO PROGRESS WOMEN INTO MANAGEMENT

Marilyn McDougall

Women in the Workforce

In the UK today, while women make up 48.9 per cent of the workforce,[1] they comprise 33 per cent of managers and administrators,[2] 4 per cent of senior managers and only 1 per cent of senior executives.[3] These figures indicate that, in spite of sex-equality legislation having been on the statute books in the UK for over twenty years, women's progress in achieving senior positions in the same proportion as men is slow.

Single-sex Training

Colwill and Vinnicombe[4] identify two broad categories into which women-in-management programmes can be distinguished: those that restrict their membership to women but address general management topics like accounting, marketing and strategy, and those that primarily address social-psychological issues facing women in the workplace and that restrict their membership to women.

The issue of whether training for women should in fact be provided on a women-only basis is one which is surrounded by some controversy, with strong views on both sides of the argument. Essentially, the argument for single-gender training for women has been based upon the unique set of problems and issues that women must face in the workplace.

14

Arguments against women-only training have been summarised as being of three kinds.[5] The first is the 'special needs' view, that somehow these special needs of women label them as different from, probably inferior to, men. Some writers stress that such training points to women being deficient in some way, and also presents women as receiving favoured treatment which men do not receive, and is thus a cause of conflict and tension between women and men.[6] The second is the 'real world' argument that, if women are to be successful managers, their training should be provided in a way which reflects the real world, namely in a mixed group with male colleagues. The third is the 'coping' argument that, if women are to learn how to work with men as their bosses, colleagues or staff, they should experience working with them on training courses.

Bargh[7] highlights the potential for trivialisation in women-only training, when she argues that since what women do has been traditionally accorded lower status than men, such benefit as women derive from special training may be more than offset by perceptions of it as being trivial. There is also the point that women do not gain as much company-sponsored training as their male counterparts; and, especially in a time of scarce resources, if such limited sponsorship is for initiatives which are perceived as 'trivial', any benefits gained may be offset by disadvantages.[8] It has also been suggested[9] that women-only training involves preaching to the converted, that the people who really need to understand key issues in women's situations are not the women themselves but others in the organisation.

On the other hand, in considering the positive side of this argument, evidence has been provided[10, 11] which reveals that all-women management groups are less threatening and that they provide a forum where women are not dominated by men in terms of either numbers or any other criterion. There is evidence that women feel that they are more able to admit faults, identify needs and engage in means of developing their strengths when they are in an all-female group.[12] As to women's minority status in many management-training situations, it has been suggested that a woman's learning can in fact be limited by the expectations held, in some instances by the trainer, or indeed by other participants in mixed training events where the woman is often in the minority.[13] In relation to gaining managerial skills, confidence-building and assertiveness training, there is also evidence[14] that women-only courses have been particularly successful in women's learning.

Clearly, therefore, there are strong arguments on both sides of this issue. As to what women themselves say, a quarter of the sample in a recent study were 'absolutely against women-only training courses of any kind, believing them to be a form of discrimination, arguing that they were too unlike the real world in organisations'.[15] Yet, in a Scottish survey of sixty organisations, it was found that attitudes towards women-only training were directly related to experience of it: those with experience took a positive view, while those without took a negative view.[16]

With regard to the provision of women-only training, a number of points are important.[17] They include the facts that women-only training must receive clearly articulated support from top management if it is to be credible; that accusations of sex discrimination may result and thus the organisation should be prepared to offer male-facilitated, men-only training to enable men to address sex-role issues in a safe environment as well; that a specific issue or a specific group of women should be targeted (for example, top-level managers/first-line supervisors) so that there is a focus in common other than solely gender; that a decision should be made on access to such programmes, such as whether participants will be nominated according to certain criteria or whether they will be self-selecting; and that it is imperative that 'women-only training should be an adjunct to, rather than substitute for, more traditional organisational and occupational training'.[18]

Topics for Women's Training

As to the nature of training and development for women, a number of areas can be identified as important, and these include career planning, confidence-building and assertiveness skills, organisational politics and stress management.

Career Planning

It is sometimes suggested that women attain management roles less frequently due to lack of ambition on their part. There is no evidence of this from the literature; quite the reverse, in fact. What is perhaps relevant is that women are often to be found in staff rather than in line roles in organisations (for example, in personnel instead of production), and that they have chosen certain sectors in the past.

There is mixed evidence of the helpfulness of career-planning training workshops. In a Scottish study in 1990 of employers and women,[19] over half of both of these groups felt that women had a training need in the area of career planning. With many organisations currently considering issues of downsizing, career-planning workshops are sometimes offered to support employees if their jobs are at risk.

Confidence-building

The point that women can experience difficulties with confidence when they perform non-traditional roles has been described as 'the culture trap'.[20] This manifests itself in the following ways: women often have low expectations of themselves due to their backgrounds and because of socialisation; they may in fact fear

17

success in non-traditional roles because of the confusion which this represents; and women often pursue a dependent or support role in relation to men at work, for example as an assistant or a secretary. Strategies to effect change in attitudes among girls at the stage of school is possibly the way to effect influence in regard to this. As to women in employment, initiatives to help individual women to recognise and value their strengths instead perhaps of concentrating on weaknesses are important.

Assertiveness Skills

Linked with the previous point, there is a need for women to develop interpersonal skills which help to offset their domination by male colleagues in meetings, discussions and debates. Assertiveness skills are also relevant as there is evidence that women are less inclined to nominate themselves for development opportunities and for promotion. This is also highlighted as a need, from evidence that women are the subject of discrimination in the UK at all stages of the employment process.[21]

Organisational Politics

Understanding of power and politics in organisations is often said to be a prerequisite to career success. There is evidence that women are less aware of this process than their male counterparts,[22] and some organisations have highlighted this as an area of need for their development, particularly at senior levels. Mentoring by a senior colleague has been reported as an important means of learning about organisational politics.[23]

Stress Management

Some women in the UK describe themselves as lacking in confidence in their managerial role, and it is sometimes suggested that this is due to the high profile and the isolation which many women at senior levels report when they have few colleagues of their gender at that level. Sources of stress which women managers report are work overload; feeling undervalued; being the boss; being assertive and confident; and attending or being unable to attend training.[24]

Current Issues in Women's Management Training and Development

In a study of twenty-four organisations which were active or interested in women's management development, various approaches to developing women managers were identified.[25] These included women-only personal development (offered by 66 per cent of the sample) and women-in-management courses (offered by 42 per cent of the sample). Also important as vehicles for women's development were networking and mentoring, from which benefits of improved self-confidence, career advice and insights into company politics were mentioned.

For all organisations offering gender-related training or development, there was an issue concerning in-company perceptions of such initiatives. Negative action by men – and indeed also by some women – had been the result of many women's initiatives, and it may be that such a reaction was the main cause of the intentions of several organisations to move away from women-only training. For advantages to women to be gained from women-focused initiatives, and for negative reactions to be minimised, an important issue is effective communication of the rationale for such initiatives with all of the relevant stakeholders, in particular line managers, women and external trainers or consultants. The role of senior management in endorsing or imparting such communication is also crucial.

Gaining appreciation by line managers of the values of equal opportunity is at the heart of much of the training work carried out by organisations which are progressive in this field. Some are currently trying to emphasise this message by effecting change in the language of titles, for example from 'equal opportunities manager' to 'adviser', to emphasise that line managers rather than equal-opportunities specialists must manage equal opportunities. However, the criticism has to be that such change is mainly cosmetic. To create a culture of equal opportunity, managers have to be clear on what is expected as their individual contribution, and senior managers must manage their colleagues and subordinates so that they behave in ways which are in line with the new culture's requirements.

In considering issues of line-manager training, it is worth recalling points from the literature on resistance to change. Plant suggests that resistance can be systematic, from lack of appropriate knowledge, information skills and managerial capacity; or it can be behavioural, from reactions, perceptions and assumptions of individuals and groups.[26] A change to a culture which provides equality of opportunity will require to address both types of resistance. It is interesting that organisations make the greatest provision for line-manager training in relation to equal opportunities for systematic issues, with 69 per cent offering training in recruitment and selection, and 44 per cent offering equal opportunities integrated into mainstream issues such as managing people; by contrast, equal-opportunity awareness training which would address behavioural resistance was offered by only 38 per cent of the sample, and by only 8 per cent for senior managers.[27]

The integration of equal-opportunity training for managers into mainstream training provides several benefits.[28] Among the most important of these is acceptability in the eyes of managers, and the perceived integration of equal opportunities as part of management training and part of the managerial role. However, a fundamental problem exists, namely that learning or change in participants may simply not occur, as managers can miss the point when equal opportunity is part of a wider subject.

On the other hand, equal-opportunity awareness training is felt to be effective in influencing attitudes and behaviour and in helping to create an appropriate supportive environment for women who have participated in personal-development programmes. In one organisation involved in integrating equal opportunity into culture-change, a two-stage approach was used, with all employees required to participate in one-day awareness training, which was then complemented by women's initiatives and line-manager training. This combination is perhaps the ideal.

The Future

While training and development opportunities for women will remain important, it is also of fundamental importance to reflect on the nature of organisational cultures in which it is hoped women will progress. Initiatives to devise a culture which values difference, and training and development for managers to support such a culture, are essential prerequisites for breaking the 'glass ceiling'.

Notes

1. Scottish Office, *Employment Trends* (Edinburgh: HMSO, 1993).
2. Labour Force Survey, 'Employees and Self-employed in Occupations', *LFS Quarterly Bulletin* (Spring 1993).
3. NEDO, *Women Managers: The Untapped Resource* (London: Kogan-Page, 1990).
4. N. Colwill and S. Vinnicombe, 'Women's Training Needs', in J. Firth-Cozens and M. A. West (eds), *Women at Work* (Buckingham: Open University Press, 1991).
5. S. Langrish, 'Assertive Training', in C. L. Cooper (ed.), *Improving Interpersonal Relations: Some Approaches to Social Skill Training* (London: Gower, 1981).
6. A. Harlan and C. Weiss, *Moving Up: Women in Managerial Careers: Third Progress Report* (Wellesley MA: Wellesley Centre for Research on Women, 1990).

7. L. Bargh, 'Awareness Raising through Training', *Journal of European Industrial Training*, 10:1 (1986), 23–7.
8. V. Hammond, 'Management Training for Women', *Journal of European Industrial Training*, 10:7 (1986), 15–22.
9. Bargh, op. cit.
10. M. J. Davidson, *Reach for the Top: A Women's Guide to Success in Business and Management* (London: Piatkus, 1985).
11. J. Beck and M. Steel, *Beyond the Great Divide* (London: Pitman, 1989).
12. Colwill and Vinnicombe, op. cit.
13. M. J. Davidson and C. L. Cooper, *Shattering the Glass Ceiling* (London: Paul Chapman, 1992).
14. P. Makin, C. Cooper and C. Cox, *Managing People at Work* (Leicester: The British Psychological Society, 1989).
15. Davidson and Cooper, op. cit.
16. SIACE, *Equity and Efficiency – Training Women for Management* (Edinburgh: Scottish Institute for Adult and Continuing Education, 1990).
17. Colwill and Vinnicombe, op. cit.
18. Ibid.
19. SIACE, op. cit.
20. Davidson and Cooper, op. cit.
21. D. L. Collinson, 'A Question of Equal Opportunities: A Survey of Staff in a Large Insurance Company', *Personnel Review*, 16 (1987), 19–29.
22. S. Hardesty and N. Jacobs, *Success and Betrayal: The Crisis of Women in Corporate America* (Toronto: Simon and Schuster, 1986).
23. D. Clutterbuck, *Everyone Needs a Mentor* (London: IPM, 1992).
24. Davidson and Cooper, op. cit.
25. M. McDougall and S. Briley, *Developing Women Managers: Current Issues and Good Practice* (Edinburgh: HMSO, 1994).
26. R. Plant, *Managing Change and Making It Stick* (London: Fontana, 1987).
27. McDougall and Briley, op. cit.
28. Ibid.

Chapter 3

◆

DEVELOPING WOMEN AS MANAGERS
TWO CASE STUDIES

Sheena Briley

Women and Work in Scotland

TRAINING 2000, the Scottish Alliance for Women's Training, was set up in 1990 as an organisation whose purpose is to support and promote training for women in Scotland. At that time, there was a great deal of discussion about the 'demographic dip' and how this would affect Scotland's workforce, and about how women could be better utilised within the labour market. Since then, discussion of the demographic dip has been overshadowed by worldwide recession, but this does not mean that the issues to do with equality in the workplace are less valid now. If anything, it means that, in an even more competitive world marketplace, employers need to be even more aware of how vital it is that they make the very best use of all their human resources.

TRAINING 2000 does this by working with employers from across the sectors and from throughout the whole of Scotland to encourage them to make investment through training in their women employees. Training for women, as part of good human-resource development which enables women to take up jobs, to return to work and to gain promotion, is closely linked to the economic success of our country.

Currently, women are concentrated in a limited range of jobs. Over half of female employment is in catering, clerical or related occupations. We are poorly represented in areas such as science, engineering and technology, and management. This segregation into less well-paid areas is best illustrated by differences in pay: despite legislation, the average working woman earns around 79 per cent of the amount earned by her male counterpart.

As stated by Marilyn McDougall in Chapter 2, women now make up 48.9 per cent of the UK workforce, yet recent figures show that women only account for about 4 per cent of senior managers and only 1 per cent of senior executives. The questions which we need to ask are: why is this so, particularly when we know that girls, on average, do better than boys at school; what are the barriers to women in management; and how can these be overcome?

The Barriers to Management

In 1992, TRAINING 2000 undertook a research project to seek answers to these questions.[1] The research team found that the three biggest barriers to women's access to jobs and training were lack of adequate childcare, low pay, and attitudes. However, if employers are to remain economically competitive into the next decade, then they must attract and retain the best people for the jobs, and of course this means women as well as men. We must therefore look at ways of breaking down these barriers, and of enabling women to compete on a level playing-field with their male colleagues for access to jobs, to training and to promotion.

Background research undertaken by Marilyn McDougall and myself for *Developing Women Managers* (1994)[2] revealed that the proportion of women in the workforce is steadily increasing, and that fundamental changes are taking place in many women's working and family lives: women in Scotland are, on average, marrying later than in the past, and are waiting longer to have children. Many women have increased expectations of what they want from their working lives. In the wider world, the introduction of the single European market at the end of 1992 and the opening-up of East European markets have highlighted the need for a highly-skilled workforce, which can only be achieved through quality education and training. These developments, linked to increasing competition from beyond Europe, the impact of new technologies and demographic and workforce changes, further emphasise this.

This competitive challenge to employers, coupled with fundamental changes in the marketplace and in the labour force, has given the impetus to some organisations to search for innovative strategies designed to improve employee performance and create competitive advantage. To live through recession, many organisations have shrunk in size, and one employee now typically has many roles to play. Working life, then, for men and women, is becoming more competitive, as organisations demand more from their employees. Linked to this, we see that management structures across the world are changing accordingly, towards 'flatter' structures, and with an emphasis on employees gaining a broad skill range.

Increasing numbers of employers are taking heed of these changes, and new styles of management are coming to the fore. The key management concepts of the 1990s are about investing in people, quality and managing diversity, all of which can contribute to bringing about organisational change. The impetus for our book was based on all of these factors, as well as on the fact that in discussions with employers it became clear to us that women's training and development into management roles was an issue which was being examined by an increasing number of employers. It also became clear that some organisations, for whom women's management training was a new departure, were repeating errors that had been made elsewhere. At a time when budgets for training are receiving particular scrutiny, and when money for women's management training and development is often difficult to justify, this seemed to us to be particularly unfortunate.

Therefore, we decided to highlight what some employers are already doing to develop women into management roles, to illustrate to others how it can be done in their own organisations, and to show what the benefits can be, as well as some of the pitfalls to avoid. We looked for organisations with forward-looking human-resource development policies when we came to put together the case studies for our book. All of the organisations, in both the public and the private sector, had recognised that they needed to make better use of their human resources, and that, in particular, women were poorly represented at managerial level, so that something needed to be done about this, in terms of good management as well as staff morale and equality of opportunity.

The following case studies are taken from our book, and are useful illustrations of what two organisations have done to attempt to break down some of the barriers to management which are outlined above.

Case Study 1: Lothian Regional Council and Women-only Training

Lothian Regional Council had a workforce of 30,000, 75 per cent of whom were women. Until the Council re-organisation in April 1996, it was one of Scotland's largest Regional Councils, with its headquarters in Scotland's capital city, Edinburgh. In 1989, it was recognised that training courses aimed specifically at women did not exist within the Council; an assertiveness-training course for women and men was offered, and then a working party was set up with members from a range of departments that were interested in running women-only courses. This was not to be just a talking shop, but rather a focus for action.

The first project took place in 1991 and consisted of a pilot 'Women into Management' course. The working party formulated objectives and put the pilot out to tender. Using external consultants, this course was run with sixteen women participants who were mainly from the working party itself. This confirmed the need for women-only training, but was too ambitious in that there were too many objectives for a two-day course to examine. As well as this, the external tutors did not fully understand the organisational culture of the Council. However, the pilot did identify immediate suggestions for two further women-only training courses: personal and career development, and assertiveness training for women only, to be run on a half-day basis to enable part-time employees to attend. The problem was how to ensure that a 'Women into Management' course would meet women's needs, and it was therefore decided to carry out a detailed training-needs analysis.

Two questionnaires were devised by the working party. One was aimed at women managers or women aspiring to be managers; the other was aimed at senior managers in order to gain their support. Fifty-one women and twenty-five senior managers (of whom one was a woman) were interviewed using the questionnaires as a guide. The analysis was carried out by trained members of the working party, and a summary of findings was presented to the departmental heads. These findings were illuminating. They indicated that women were not applying for posts; that there was a lack of opportunity; and that women felt that they lacked experience, training and, above all, confidence. It was agreed therefore, that there was indeed a need to raise the profile and confidence of women workers within the Council, and it was decided to design an appropriate training course to meet this need, called 'Developing Management Skills for Women'. There was considerable demand for this course, which became well supported and recognised by managers. It covered three days, with a half-day follow-up later.

Other courses provided for women included 'Personal and Career Development', based on the Springboard Workbook,[3] which encourages networking. It examined such topics as assertiveness, goal-setting, planning and confidence-building, and took place over a four-month period for groups of twelve to fourteen women. It involved the individual women studying the workbook alone and then meeting formally with the other participants and tutors for a total of three full days out of the four months. In addition, informal contact and exchange of ideas were encouraged. Over seventy women had participated by the time the council was re-organised.

'Assertiveness Skills for Women' was run on a half-day basis to attract part-time staff, most of whom were women, although it was not successful in doing this. It was clear, however, that the women who did attend did so because the course was for women only. These courses were essentially about personal development rather than being job-specific. They concerned the culture of the organisation and how individuals could succeed in that culture.

The Council cited a number of benefits of offering training for women only. These included the fact that delegates were able to discuss ideas without feeling threatened; that delegates looked positively at the skills they had, which may have been neglected in the past; and that delegates began applying for jobs, training opportunities and promotion. Excellent networking resulted from some courses, although this was not an explicit objective. The process of data-collection and interviewing senior managers helped working-party members, who identified and improved their own skills, and raised their confidence and profile through this process. The concept of women-only training courses became accepted within the Council, whose organisational culture began to change. 'Training isn't going to alter the organisation by itself', said one employee; 'however, it can raise expectations which may start to alter things'.

The Council eventually gained a larger pool of internal candidates who applied for job vacancies, and more women started applying for posts. There was a clear and growing demand for places on the courses, which also raised the training expectations of male staff, who did not have access to such specific training courses of this type.

The Council also encountered some problems: organisational barriers had to be overcome, often by working as unobtrusively as possible. The expertise of external trainers was limited in helping delegates to understand the organisational culture. Some delegates wished to use the sessions as a 'moaning or complaining' forum, and some senior women objected to the courses. It was felt that such courses raised expectations about organisational success and job prospects, which could lead to problems if expectations could not be realised. It was felt that some women-only programmes suggest that women are 'separate' from men and have 'special needs'; but this is a notion that many women wish to dispel.

The way forward for the Council was to offer further training, including a new course, 'Foundation Management Skills for Women', designed to meet an emerging need to provide a bridge between the 'Personal and Career Development' course and the 'Developing Management Skills for Women' course. There were also plans to develop personal development-based skills training for men and women with the provisional title of 'Developing Personal Effectiveness as a Manager'. Networking was organised by participants of the 'Developing Management Skills for Women' course, with the aim of developing in local government. An equal-opportunities module in a management competence programme was being developed.

Case Study 2: The Royal Bank of Scotland–Incorporating Equal Opportunities into Mainstream Training

An Equal Opportunities Committee within the Royal Bank of Scotland was formed in 1987, and since then policies and guidelines have been developed and implemented. Although a Manager for Equal Opportunities was appointed in 1989, the title was recently changed to 'adviser' with the intention of making line managers more aware of their ownership of equal opportunities. Since 1989, the proportion of women in management roles has increased as shown in Table 3.1.

TABLE 3.1:   The proportion of women in management roles, 1989 and 1993.

	1989 (%)	1993 (%)
Women assistant managers	22.0	32.0
Women managers	2.5	9.2
Women senior managers	0.0	2.2
Women executives	0.0	2.4

The Bank sees a variety of benefits in integrating equal opportunities into mainstream training, and these are described as follows: that equal opportunities is not seen a separate issue, but is a part of everything that the Royal Bank does; that such an approach demonstrates commitment, and shows that the subject is taken seriously; and that if the subject is being addressed from various perspectives, it shows commitment to making equality of opportunity a reality. Importantly, the business reasons are emphasised: in mainstream training, the point that there is a business case for equal opportunities can be made, otherwise it can be seen as a soft option and not a business case. Overall, this sort of equality training is part of the cultural change that is happening within the Royal Bank: the organisation is seeking to create and develop a more open and honest culture.

The Bank experienced some problems with putting this training into practice. The primary problem was that the trainers were not equal-opportunities specialists, could therefore only give a limited amount of information, and needed guidance on where to obtain further information if they did not have it themselves. There was also felt to be a lack of ownership by line management, and whether or not managers had the concept 'on board' varied widely. There also seemed to be a perceived lack of commitment from senior levels. If the commitment is not demonstrated at the top, then confidence in this issue is lost.

For the Royal Bank of Scotland, future plans included piloting a Springboard Training Programme,[4] as well as single-gender training. The Royal Bank believed that it was still difficult to 'sell' the concept of single-gender training to line managers. Other organisations which have used single-gender training with positive outcomes could act as useful examples. The Royal Bank was committed to investigating other training options, and felt that mandatory awareness training, extended to all line managers, could be beneficial.

These case studies are just two examples of how and why two major employers chose to use positive action in training to develop women as managers within their organisations. An increasing number of organisations are investigating and initiating innovative human-resource development policies in order to remain competitive. Both of the organisations highlighted here believe that the training initiatives which they put into place have been to their benefit in terms of good management, since good human-resource development is an essential component of any good management system.

Notes

1. TRAINING 2000 (Scotland) Ltd, *Women's Access to Jobs and Skills* (Scottish Enterprise/Highlands and Islands Enterprise, 1992).
2. M. McDougall and S. Briley, *Developing Women Managers: Current Issues and Good Practice* (Edinburgh: HMSO, 1994).
3. L. Willis and J. Daisley, *Springboard Women's Development Workbook* (Hawthorn Press, 1990).
4. Ibid.

Part 2

Women and Training in Rural Communities Around the World

Chapter 4

◆

Raising Entrepreneurial Awareness
Some Issues Relating to Rural Women

Christina Hartshorn

Social change can take two forms. It can be spontaneous, without deliberate planning, and/or as a reaction to events over greater or shorter time-spans; or it can be engineered by groups or combinations of groups in society, such as government or pressure/interest groups, to achieve specific goals. An example of this second form of social change is a campaign to raise women's awareness of enterprise. Kotler and Roberto[1] describe a social-change campaign as 'an organised effort conducted by one group (the change agent) which intends to persuade others (the target adopters) to accept, modify or abandon certain ideas, attitudes, practice and behaviour'. Social-change campaigns may have more than one set of target adopters.

This chapter describes such a social-change campaign, using a framework first suggested by Kotler and Roberto. They suggest that there are five core elements to a social-change campaign:

Cause: a social goal which will provide a solution to a social need or problem.

Change agent: a group, or individuals, acting as a catalyst to effect social change.

Target adopters: any persons or groups, including government, whose attitudes and behaviours are the object of the desired change.

Channels: the pathways through which the social-change

| | message is communicated to the target adopters and feedback is received by the change agent. |
| *Change strategy:* | the total plan devised by the change agent to achieve the identified social-change objectives. |

Raising Entrepreneurial Awareness in Women

The Women's Enterprise Unit is located within the Scottish Enterprise Foundation. It was created in 1986 against a background of under-representation of women as business owners, and its aim is 'to encourage and enable more women in Scotland to take up business ownership and be more effective in that ownership'.[2] The Unit can therefore be seen as a *change agent*.

Despite the fact that female self-employment has increased rapidly over the last ten years in Scotland as in many other western economies, the female share of the total population of self-employed is actually declining (see Table 4.1). As national statistics show, far fewer women are self-employed than men, and the percentage of female self-employment is generally lower in Scotland than in any other region of mainland Britain (see Table 4.2).

There are a number of factors which contribute to the lower numbers of women in self-employment. A significant proportion of the female population are economically inactive due to full-time domestic commitments. It is difficult to target measures of enterprise support, such as information, advice and training, to those women who are home-based. They are socially isolated and are not linked into conventional networks through which information and support could be channelled.

Research has shown that previous work experience in the proposed line of business can be a key to venture success. In this

TABLE 4.1:   Number of females in self-employment as a percentage of total self-employment in Scotland.

	1983 No. (000s)	%	1987 No. (000s)	%	1988 No. (000s)	%	1989 No. (000s)	%
Female S.E.	42	23.46	42	21.65	46	21.39	48	20.33
Total S.E.	179		194		215		236	

Source: *Employment Gazette,* June 1990.

TABLE 4.2:   Female self-employment as a percentage of total self-employment by region, 1989.

Region	Percentage
Scotland	20.3
North Yorkshire & Humberside	25.8
West Midlands	27.0
East Anglia	27.0
Wales	26.0
North-West	26.0
East Midlands	24.0
South-West	26.5
South-East	23.8

Source: Scottish Enterprise Foundation, 1992.

respect, women as a group are at a disadvantage, as they are concentrated in low-skilled occupations.[3] Few women, therefore, hold managerial positions where they could learn the management skills necessary for running a business.[4] In addition, the fostering of a successful business idea is restricted by limited work experience. Indeed, this may in turn lead women towards low-skilled self-employment.[5]

Another factor preventing women from entering self-employment is their perception of themselves, which is still dominated by traditional stereotypes.[6] Research into female entrepreneurship has highlighted women's lack of confidence and assertiveness. This can affect women at all stages of business development, but may be a fatal inhibition at the pre-start-up stage when a woman may feel particularly vulnerable about the viability of her business idea.[7]

The *social problem* in question, therefore, is the low rate of participation by women in business ownership or enterprise and how to increase it. The social objective is to help overcome the problem by raising women's awareness of enterprise as an economic option that is available to them. To date, public campaigns to encourage wider participation in business ownership have used general messages supported by male images and vocabulary. Low number of women business owners mean that there are fewer relevant and accessible role models available to women who are at the pre-start-up stage.

Without positive messages and direct targeting to raise self-confidence, it is difficult for women to perceive themselves as potential business owners who will successfully overcome the specific barriers outlined above. Women are thus identified as one group of *target adopters*.

Scotland has a fairly sophisticated but uneven enterprise support network consisting of both public and private providers of information, advice and resources. A key local delivery point for enterprise support is the Enterprise Trust. Each Trust is funded and managed locally by a mix of public and private organisations. There are forty-one Trusts in Scotland, each working independently but in loose collaboration with others under an umbrella organisation, Scottish Business in the Community.

The geographical sparsity of Enterprise Trusts makes it difficult for them to support the entrepreneur, potential or actual, consistently throughout Scotland. Many areas of rural Scotland in particular are disadvantaged through geographic isolation. In Central/Lowland Scotland, no member of the public is more than about ten to fifteen miles from a Trust, whereas in the Highlands and Borders the figure is closer to fifty miles. Women are doubly disadvantaged: in addition to general isolating factors, public transport in rural areas has all but disappeared, and, even when a household does own a car, it is usual for the male to have sole access in order to reach his place of employment. Women are therefore effectively denied access to sources of enterprise information and advice.

Enterprise Trusts and all other enterprise support organisations are staffed almost exclusively by men. Research, however, has indicated that female business counsellors are an important source of support during the very early stages of enterprise creation.[8] Further research[9] has shown that the majority of the enterprise support network in Scotland adopts a gender-blind approach to its work. Gender-blindness is a state which denies any difference between male and female clients in terms of experience and background, and therefore denies any difference in terms of needs.[10] This gender-blindness is due to a lack of providers' awareness of the distinct needs of women. Other studies in Europe[11] have reported unfavourable treatment of women by financiers and bankers; and, while in the UK evidence is extremely difficult to find, women's *perceptions* of their treatment by male business advisers have often been reported as 'patronising'.[12]

A more positive set of attitudes and behaviours by enterprise advisers towards women would lower the awareness barrier. A second group of *target adopters* in the social-change campaign would therefore be business advisers. The Women's Enterprise Unit decided in 1988 to act as a catalyst for social change and mount a campaign to raise women's awareness of enterprise.[13] The specific objectives of the campaign were:

1. to raise women's awareness of the option of self-employment;
2. to raise the awareness of the enterprise support network of the particular needs of women;
3. to raise the profile of women business owners in order to encourage positive attitudes towards women's potential contribution to the economy.

Developing the Campaign

The change strategy for achieving these objectives needed, in part, to bring together the two sets of target adopters, female potential entrepreneurs and business advisers. Furthermore, the campaign was required to have a high profile if positive attitudes regarding women in business were to be fostered among the community at large. The following three factors were of significant importance.

First, a major barrier for women, especially those in rural areas, was access to enterprise information. In order to lower the 'access to information' barrier, it was determined that the enterprise awareness campaign should be taken *to the women* in places where they lived and shopped. This could have been via the mail, or by means of posters; but a more effective method of promotion[14] is through personal communication. Second, it was crucial that the first group of target adopters (women) should understand that the campaign was directed specifically and solely towards them. An unambiguous message therefore had to be constructed.

Third, the second set of target adopters (business advisers) had little experience of interviewing potential women entrepreneurs. The fewer women seen by an adviser, the more difficult it is for him to break free from rigidly stereotyping women. Formal business networks such as Rotary and Chambers of Commerce are, in the main, run by men with men in mind. It was therefore paramount to use women as core staff for the enterprise awareness campaign, to act as positive role models. However, it was equally important to introduce male business advisers to a large number of potential female clients in order to help them to discover the *actual* needs of this client group.

The Women's Enterprise Unit therefore decided to use a mobile facility to channel the 'enterprise option' message of the campaign. This would allow the message, namely business start-up information and advice, to be taken to the women target group. A double-decker bus was chosen as the mobile facility, as it was large enough to provide both impersonal exhibition space and also confidential advice and counselling areas. The elements of the campaign's marketing mix are summarised in Figure 4.1.

Product

The offer made to the two sets of target adopters was the social idea that women in Scotland should be presented with impartial advice, to allow them to make an informed choice about business ownership as an economic option. The product was targeted particularly at women returners, as they were identified as a hitherto untapped source of entrepreneurs and a group difficult to reach through conventional marketing methods.

Price

There was no monetary cost to the women, nor was there any obligation to engage in discussions with roadshow staff. The message that entry to the bus was free was heavily stressed. There was also little opportunity cost to the women, as they could come aboard without pre-booking and could stay for however long they wished.

Figure 4.1   The 4 + 3 - P social marketing mix.

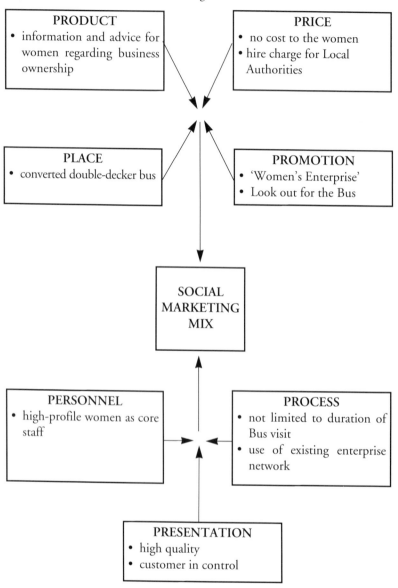

Source: Adapted by the author from Kotler and Roberto (1989), *Social Marketing*, p. 44.

There was a pricing policy as far as the second target group was concerned. The Women's Enterprise Roadshow campaign was funded by a mix of public and private sponsorship. Capital costs of bus hire, bus conversion and core staff salaries were met by national government. Running costs were met by charging local authorities a hiring fee on a daily or weekly basis. The roadshow was planned within a context of an increasing awareness by the enterprise support sector that women could form a new entrepreneurial source. This sector was aware that its services to date had in general not attracted women clients, and was thus extremely receptive to a well-formulated and well-managed offer from an experienced and reputable external agent. Demand from local authorities was so heavy that every day of the twelve-week campaign was booked, and some organisations' requirements could not be met.

Place

The use of a converted double-decker bus meant that the product could be delivered to the women in their own towns and villages, so lowering the 'access to information' barrier imposed by geographical isolation. Local business advisers augmented the core personnel. They were able to meet these new female clients in an informal setting, away from a potentially threatening formal office. The telephone installed on the bus ensured that the follow-up appointments could be made on the spot, with no time delay. The location of the bus within a particular town was critical. The most effective locations were in pedestrian areas and near shopping centres on main thoroughfares.

Promotion

The campaign logo 'Women's Enterprise' was chosen to alert women to the fact that the roadshow was *for them*. Experience of a previous event in Glasgow showed that three times the anticipated number of women had attended a 'Women's Enterprise Awareness Week'[15] than similar non-gender-specific events. Enterprise was used as a loose concept to denote the promotion of working for oneself rather than for an employer. It included self-employment and also business ownership employing others.

The outside of the bus was designed to attract attention and to publicise both the roadshow itself and the concept of Women in Enterprise. The roadshow message, 'Women's Enterprise', delivered on the outside of the bus, was unchanging throughout the tour, 'to anchor the campaign and [to give] it a consistent identity',[16] unlike the exhibition and displays inside, which changed with each location to reflect local services.

There was a supplementary advertising and public-relations campaign to publicise the concept, but more specifically to alert potential target adopters to when and where the bus would be in their area. Press releases were dispatched to local press two weeks prior to the arrival of the bus. The message 'delivering the enterprise option' was featured in all press releases to ensure a consistency of approach throughout the country, while 10,000 posters displaying a colourful graphic of the bus and inviting women to 'Look out for the Bus' were printed and distributed in advance via the enterprise support sector. There was a blank space for the addition of local timings and venues. These posters were displayed on banks' premises and in public buildings.

Some publicity through local radio was also achieved. Matching 'stickers' with the roadshow logo were stuck to all items of literature taken away by the women clients as a post-event 'prompt'.

Personnel

The campaign policy was that the two core roadshow staff were to be high-profile, high-status women. Research has indicated that female business counsellors are an important source of support for women at the awareness/pre-start-up stage of business creation.[17] The roadshow manager was a senior bank manager on secondment from Bank of Scotland who acted as a positive role model for both sets of adopters. She was an example of a successful woman professional who well understood the problems voiced by the women who came on board. She was also an example to the business advisers of a female with an equal if not superior status to themselves.

The coordinator had further qualifications and experience in information technology and was able to present business information and advice via on-board computers. Both women presented a positive and welcoming presence to the female target adopters who came on board.

The male business advisers had immediate local knowledge of markets and services available. They were exposed to the issues raised from a female perspective and were able to discuss them in both general and specific terms with the core female staff.

Presentation

The roadshow vehicle was designed both outside and inside to impart a sense of informality, warmth and encouragement. The fixtures and fittings were of a high quality, and the layout was designed to allow visitors to retain control rather than feel intimidated by staff or swamped by information.

Process

The steps taken by the target adopters to acquire the social idea were not confined or limited to the duration of the bus being in one particular place. Taking the four-stage 'AIDA' model, we can review the process of 'choosing the enterprise option'. For women, the first necessary stage is *awareness,* that business ownership exists as an economic activity and is open to them. The aim of the Women's Enterprise Roadshow was to raise their level of awareness. The second or *interest* stage takes women beyond awareness to wanting to know more about it, such as how to get started and what the requirements are. The staff on board the bus could give this information to a high degree of detail. Progressing through to the stage of *desiring* the option, a woman visitor could take the decision while on board the bus to become a business owner. The third stage would, however, be more likely to occur after her visit to the roadshow, when translating the desire to become a business owner into reality was greatly enhanced by the presence of the local business adviser.

He could book a follow-up appointment, refer her to a specialist professional or register her on a business start-up course. The use of the bus as a mechanism to link business advisers to potential clients ensured that an *action* channel was open whenever the client chose to use it. Social marketing has to be underpinned with a sense of social responsibility. If its aim is to persuade people to change their attitudes and behaviours, then one must ensure that the final product can be delivered. The inclusion of local business advisers in the campaign ensured that when the roadshow moved to its next location, the delivery mechanism was still in place.

On the Road

The Women's Enterprise Roadshow toured mainland Scotland for twelve weeks during the autumn of 1989. It followed a geographically logical route which attempted to cover the most distant rural locations before the onset of the limited daylight and poor weather which is experienced in the latter part of the year. All nine regions of mainland Scotland were covered, with a total of seventy-two locations visited. The bus was open to visitors on average five days a week from between 9 and 10 a.m. until between 5 and 7 p.m. It was also open on eight Saturdays and Sundays.

The lower deck of the bus was converted to an exhibition centre comprising display boards which also contained local information. Racks containing a range of literature were positioned to allow clients to browse and make their own selection. Various sponsors provided the roadshow with general literature on business start-up, business planning and presentation of the business plan. Other literature contained local and more specialised information.

The upper deck had additional display boards which showed details of the business services offered by the roadshow sponsors. There were video facilities on both decks which were used to show promotional videos of a Region or short instructional videos on business start-up. Personal computers with a range of business software were also available on both decks.

One sponsor provided a series of finance workshops presented by female accountants. On the whole, the flow of women visitors through the bus proved to be too erratic to allow static presentation. Most women preferred to talk to a business adviser on an individual basis; so, instead of going ahead with the presentations, the female accountants responded to the visitors' actual needs and acted in an individual advisory capacity on financial matters.

Involvement of Target Adopters
Women

Over 1,000 women came on board the bus. The event provided an opportunity to collect data on the hitherto little-recorded group of women potential entrepreneurs. A short questionnaire was completed by business advisers and roadshow staff on behalf of 935 women visitors. Information was collected about the individual, her business idea and her information needs.

Contrary to expectations, the overwhelming majority of visitors to the roadshow already had an idea for a business. It had been assumed that the target adopters, women in the very early stages of thinking about business ownership, would have only a generalised notion of enterprise, and that this stage would precede the acquisition of a business idea. It can be determined from these data whether the women with a specific business idea had already progressed through a more general stage, or whether they had an idea first and had come to ascertain whether they themselves could and/or should build a business based on that idea.

What can be concluded is that a great number of women with business ideas had done nothing to develop their idea using the existing enterprise support structure. Also to the organisers' surprise, almost 10 per cent of the visitors were already in business, but chose to come to the roadshow for information and advice rather than use existing enterprise facilities. It was not possible to ascertain whether this was because of opportunism or as a response to previous negative experiences, but certainly a mobile business information centre is also attractive to existing business owners.

Business Sector Choice

The choice of business sector was compared with the UK picture to see if there was any variance. The national population of women self-employed is concentrated in two main service sectors,[18] namely distribution, hotels and catering; and other services. Similarly, from the roadshow visitors, nearly three-quarters of potential business ideas recorded were in the service sector (see Table 4.3), the highest proportion (32 per cent) being in distribution, hotels and catering. Women business owners in this sector are more likely to employ staff than owners in the 'other services' sector. There is considerable scope for job creation, therefore, among these potential women business owners.

TABLE 4.3: Stages of entrepreneurial development.

	Women who had no specific business idea		Women who had a specific business idea		Women who already run their own business	
	No.	%	No.	%	No.	%
Total	194	21.3	629	69.0	88	9.6

Source: Scottish Enterprise Foundation, 1992.

Previous research has shown that women entrepreneurs tend to be restricted in their choice of business by employment experience and adherence to traditional domestic roles.[19, 20] In addition, ease of market entry may influence their sectoral choice. These factors combine to limit women entrepreneurs often to low-profit, high-risk service businesses with restricted growth potential.

Evidence from the roadshow shows a significant number of manufacturing business ideas (23.8 per cent). This is due to a preponderance of craft, textile and clothing businesses. The overall picture of the roadshow respondents shows a greater interest in manufacturing and a lower interest in services than the national average for female self-employment in the UK (see Table 4.4). If such albeit small-scale manufacturing businesses were encouraged to develop, this would help to create more sustainable businesses which could contribute to the local economy.

The specific business ideas from the women visitors can be grouped into ten categories within the two sectors, as follows:

TABLE 4.4: Sector by standard industrial classification source.

Sector	Potential Business		Existing Business		Female Self-employed in Great Britian in 1989	
	No.	%	No.	%	No.	%
Agriculture/Fisheries	16	2.5	6	6.8	28	3.7
Metal Goods Engineering Vechicle Industry	0	0	0	0	7	0.9
*Other Manufacturing Industries	150	23.8	25	28.4	48	6
Construction	0	0	0	0	17	2.3
Distribution Hotels/Catering	204	32.4	13	14.7	271	36
Transport/ Communications	6	0.9	1	1.1	13	2
Banking/Financial/ Insurance Business Services	80	12.7	12	13.6	90	12
Other Services	173	27.5	31	35.2	279	37
Total	629	99.8	88	99.8	754	99.9

Source: Labour Force Survey, 1989.

Manufacturing sector
- craft businesses
- textile and clothing manufacturers

Service sector
- traditional care businesses (reflecting the traditional role of women as carers of the young and the elderly), e.g. creches, nurseries, homes for the elderly
- retail
- catering

- recreational and personal services
- business support services
- farming and livestock (sixteen of these businesses were in the agricultural sector)
- tourism
- miscellaneous

Type of Advice Sought

Broadly speaking, it can be seen that women came to the roadshow seeking both general advice and specific business advice. These types of advice were not mutually exclusive, however, and a woman may have requested both start-up advice and specific advice about premises, for instance. As Table 4.5 shows, the highest proportion (43 per cent) of enquiries were requests for specific business advice. One third were about start-up advice, and about a quarter of the enquiries were of a general nature.

TABLE 4.5:   Level of advice sought.

| | General Enquiry | | Start-up | | Specific Advice | | Total | |
	No.	%	No.	%	No.	%	No.	%
Total	270	24	396	32.2	484	43.0	1123	99.2

Source: Scottish Enterprise Foundation, 1992.

General Enquiries

Enquiries of a general nature ranged from questions of confidence ('Do you think I've got the know-how to run a business?' 'It's just an idea I've had; what do you think about it?') to careers counselling ('Am I better working for someone else than trying to work for myself?' 'I trained as a chiropodist; do you think I can make a go of it on my own?'). Women were looking for general support and encouragement to help them to move forwards. They were seeking frameworks to help them evaluate alternative courses of action, and a recognition from 'professionals' that their business idea, or general desire to run a business, was valid and worthwhile.

Start-up Advice

Start-up advice was generally given when the enquirer had a business idea but was uncertain of what to do next and had done no market research or other research into its viability. It involved giving a 'Route into Business' context, advice on how to conduct market research and the rudiments of writing a business plan.

Specific Advice

Requests for specific advice were common throughout the campaign (see Table 4.6). For women who were thinking of starting a business, the type of specific advice requested most frequently (33 per cent) concerned the financial-control aspects of a business. The reason for this may be a general anxiety about 'red tape'.[21] It may also reflect concern about lack of experience in the technical or mechanical aspects of running a business.

TABLE 4.6: Specific advice requested.

	Financial		Grants		Marketing		Training		Premises		Expansion	
	No.	%	No.	%	No.	%	No.	%	No.	%	No.	%
Total	160	33	95	19.6	91	18.8	70	14.5	37	7.6	31	6

Source: *Employment Gazette*, June 1990.

The next most frequent request (19 per cent) was for information about grants and loans. In total, these two categories form over half of all requests for specific advice. This supports evidence from previous research which shows women's perception of 'finance' as being a barrier to business start-up.[22]

Conventional 'steps into business' teaching is based on a marketing orientation, that is, businesses are formed around meeting a market need. The low frequency of requests for advice on marketing (18 per cent) in comparison to those for finance (52 per cent) raised certain issues, in particular: are women aware of the importance of marketing in small business? Do women have to break through the 'finance perception' barrier before they can consider whether their business idea is viable? Is women's awareness of marketing issues so high that they do not need to ask advice? These questions can only be answered by further research into the area.

Business Advisers

In total, approximately 150 individual business advisers staffed the roadshow. Some were employed by the private sector, but a slight majority were from the public sector. The level of enthusiasm demonstrated by the business advisers was very high. A useful outcome of the event was that business advisers working in any given area often met for the first time on board the bus. Thus the private and public sectors had an opportunity to work with a common purpose towards a common end. The roadshow acted as a catalyst to forge local networks of business advisers.

The permanent presence of senior female bankers and accountants acted to help male business advisers to reshape their attitudes towards women clients. Many follow-up actions and activities for women have been undertaken by male advisers subsequent to the roadshow. The private-sector advisers were able to gather qualitative data concerning how women view their products and services, feeding back this market research to their companies. There has been a considerable rise in the gender-awareness of private-sector companies as seen in the language, imagery and orientation of their current business literature.

Policymakers

One of the aims of this social-change campaign was to encourage the participation of the entrepreneurial support network. Comprising mainly public-sector organisations, it responded overwhelmingly to the roadshow as follows: 66 per cent of Regional Councils participated; 75 per cent of District Councils participated; and 95 per cent of Enterprise Trusts participated.

Prior to the roadshow, awareness of Enterprise Trusts (the principal deliverer of local enterprise advice, information and services) among women had been very low. Very few visitors to the bus had heard of them, and were even less likely to be familiar with their services. The campaign acted as a very effective marketing tool for the Enterprise Trust movement. This focused initiative ensured that, at the policy level, organisations agreed that more women should be helped into business, and they coordinated their efforts and activities to ensure a positive outcome.

Promotional Methods

Mobile delivery of goods and services is a familiar concept to women in rural Scotland. Locally, most rural areas have mobile fishmongers and mobile libraries. At a national level, the Scottish Arts Council has a pantechnicon which takes exhibitions of art to rural communities. In all areas of Scotland, people are familiar with the Mobile Blood Donor Service and readily enter the trailer to donate blood.

It was anticipated that there would be a high rate of opportunistic attendance to the roadshow, which was in fact the case (see Table 4.7). The most successful method of attracting women onto the bus was to have it located centrally, for example in pedestrian areas near shopping centres. The aggregate data presented in Table 4.7, however, mask the divergent responses reported in some areas. For example, in a former industrial town in the central belt of Scotland, which had previously been highly industrialised, there was a very poor attendance rate among women. Potential visitors were seen viewing the bus but not coming on board.

TABLE 4.7: Promotional methods.

	Number of women	%
Noticed the bus as they were passing	396	42
Read about it in the press	293	31
Heard from another source	118	12
Seen a poster	58	6
Heard from someone else	42	4.5
Heard about it on the radio	28	3

Source: Scottish Enterprise Foundation, 1992.

The Local Enterprise Trust business adviser (female) undertook a follow-up investigation. Her respondents reported negative attitudes concerning the upmarket, high-quality image portrayed by the bus. Its appearance and message were not appropriate or accessible to the women of this 'traditional' community. 'Women's Enterprise' was too obscure a message, and the University of Stirling crest on the driver's door also proved discouraging. The Enterprise Trust adviser felt that the 'mobile advice and information' concept would be appropriate with some adjustments to suit local needs. She therefore hired another bus herself, with a medium-quality image and a much more general 'Women back to Work' message. In her local area, this proved to meet the needs of women returners, with many scores of women attending.

The Rural Perspective

The issues from the campaign which have particular relevance to women's enterprise in rural areas can be grouped into two sets, namely those issues which are external to the client and those which are internal to the client.

External Issues

External issues are the attitudes of others and issues of access to information regarding enterprise, which is restricted by geographic isolation. This inaccessibility is compounded by lack of access to public or private transport, and by the time constraints imposed by domestic and family responsibilities. Access to enterprise advice may be limited by the likely help available. Prevailing reference-group norms may further reinforce the belief that business self-help groups (Rotary, etc.) are a male-only preserve. The lack of alternative sources of advice in smaller communities further acts as a barrier.

Women who used the roadshow consistently used limiting phrases to describe their business idea or themselves: 'it's *only* an idea'; 'it's *just* a notion I've had'. At the very early stages of enterprise development, clients need much more personal support and enthusiasm from advisers, to help them to develop themselves and their ideas to a logical resolution. If women perceive a less-than-positive attitude from business advisers, bankers and financiers, they are easily discouraged.

Attitudes of family and friends may also be discouraging. In more traditional societies, there may be structural subservience. Infrastructures are built around traditional sex roles, where women are at home managing the home while men are out of the home for most of the day at work. While business information and advice may not be denied to a woman (Sex Discrimination Act 1975, and as revised 1986), underlying attitudes cannot be the subject of legislation.

There is a general lack of relevant entrepreneurial role models for women. This is exacerbated in rural communities, whose smaller populations limit women's opportunities to see other, local women as business owners. A rural woman may also have more limited access to markets for her business, and her ideas may be similarly restricted. It may be more difficult to conduct market research, especially searches from secondary sources usually found only in large libraries.

Internal Issues

Internal issues comprise confidence, self-concept and skills. Lack of confidence through years away from the workforce is widely regarded as a barrier common to many women contemplating business ownership. Training in groups and networking with other women is a proven method to rebuild confidence. While distance learning materials are proving invaluable in rural areas as a means to improve or extend general education, geographic isolation is a barrier to women taking up group training activities.

The self-concept of the potential woman entrepreneur is formulated within an existing role-set and value-set. There are fewer opportunities in rural areas than in urban locations to join networks of aspiring or actual business owners to expand, develop or test out alternative concepts of the self as business owner. It has been recognised[23] that this process of affective socialisation is critical to the successful adoption and execution of the role of the small business owner. Conversely, the need for self-reliance experienced by many rural women may prove beneficial in the demands imposed by the isolated nature of business ownership.

Where women have lived in smaller rural communities all their lives, their general exposure to the world of work and commerce is lower, and their specific occupational experience is more restricted than that of women who live in urban settings. There are fewer job opportunities at all levels, and fewer face-to-face training opportunities.

Wider Applications

The Women's Enterprise Roadshow is an example of social campaign to change public attitudes and behaviour. The bus was the outward manifestation of the campaign, but it was only one element in the total strategy.

Social-change campaigns have a long historical provenance and are not confined to any particular culture. Anti-slavery campaigns were recorded in Ancient Greece; AIDS awareness campaigns are currently sponsored by such diverse organisations as the Norwegian government and private farm owners in Zimbabwe. Adapting campaigns for use in other cultures, or for different target adopters, must be undertaken cautiously, and a number of elements must be reviewed.

The *social goal* must be clearly identified. Often there will be an unquantifiable broad objective, such as 'conserving energy', 'raising the standard of life' or 'improving economic opportunities for women'. The short-term goals, however, must be specific, measurable, attainable, relevant and trackable ('SMART') if there is to be any evaluation of the campaign. For example, mass literacy campaigns can measure absolute levels of literacy, changes in levels and the time taken to raise levels. A social change has a greater chance of adoption the more congruent it is with an audience's prior set of attitudes.[24, 25]

A detailed knowledge of *local environmental factors* is especially important when targeting social-change campaigns to isolated rural groups. An important set of factors is the prevailing sociocultural forces, including existing attitudes towards, say, working for oneself, or women working outside the home or in paid employment anywhere. Lazarsfeld and Merton (1949)[26] identified the importance of 'monopolisation', that is, that there should be no contrary messages to that of the social-change campaign if success is to be assured. In isolated societies, there are often powerful individuals who have vested interests that are contrary to those of the social-change goals. For example, in the recent literacy campaign in West Bengal, it was common to find intransigent attitudes among landowners who did not wish their labourers to learn how to read and write. These negative attitudes formed a powerful barrier to be surmounted by illiterate workers in the pursuit of reading skills.

These powerful and influential people may be identified as a *secondary target adopter group* for whom a separate but parallel social-change campaign has to be organised. This increases the chances of successful adoption of the new social goals by the primary target adopters. For example, in a recent health campaign mounted by the BBC World Service, a village elder's wife is heard to visit a mobile cervical-cancer testing unit. This gives a seal of approval to the campaign, and the character acts as a role model to other women, dispelling any misconceptions or fears that might be held among the target adopters.

There must be a *clear identification of target adopters*. For example, following the end of the Second World War, there was a chronic food shortage in the UK, and the Ministry of Agriculture wanted to improve food production. The strategy employed was to target farmers and their families with information about new methods, crops, advisory services etc. This was relayed via radio entertainment at times when families would be sitting together relaxing, such as during or after meals. The radio soap opera *The Archers* has been broadcast daily for over forty years, and a recent 'information input' contained details of enterprise for women. Two characters, farmers' wives, are generating income through extensions of farming activities, namely bed-and-breakfast holidays on a working farm, and ice-cream and frozen yoghurts from organically-produced milk.

The *change strategy* itself should take into account the factors identified above. In particular, it should be congruent with prevailing cultures in terms of methods of promotion, vocabulary and delivery. Intrinsically bound with this is the *message* itself. Questions of whether it should be universal or specific can only be answered in relation to the heterogeneity of the target adopting group. The message has to be phrased in terms that highlight the benefits of the social product or idea to the target adopters, rather than its features.

Target groups either have a problem to solve, or they have needs and wants which they wish to satisfy. Business ownership can be presented as the solution to low family income or low job satisfaction, or a means of reconciling either of the previous solutions with other family demands. Business ownership can also be the means of satisfying the need for a higher family income (for general or specific purposes), for creativity or for the wide-ranging 'need to achieve'.

Promotional methods need to be familiar to the target adopters. Buses are a regular feature of daily life in Britain, so the promotional message was not lost in an unfamiliar setting. Two popular methods of transmitting 'messages' in rural India are by means of puppet shows and street theatre. The West Bengal literacy campaign, referred to above, used street theatre to promote the benefits of literacy. The scenario enacted also prompted anti-superstition messages. The People's Science Movement in Kerala used puppets to encourage target adopters to view science as accessible and relevant to their daily lives. These promotional methods, in common with the bus used in the Women's Enterprise Roadshow, form only part of a total social-change strategy. Carefully and appropriately chosen, however, they can have a profound impact on the extent to which any social-change campaign is successful.

Acknowledgements

This chapter was originally presented to the Regional Workshop on Women's Microenterprises, Ahmedabad, 4–7 August 1992.

Notes

1. P. Kotler and E. Roberto, *Social Marketing* (New York: The Free Press, 1989).
2. Women's Enterprise Unit.
3. C. Hakim, *Occupational Segregation: A Comparative Study of the Degree and Pattern of the Differentiation between Men's and Women's Work in Britain. the United States and Other Countries,* Research Paper no. 9 (London: Department of Employment, 1979).
4. V. Beechey, 'Women's Employment in Contemporary Britain', in V. Beechey and E. Whitelegg (eds), *Women in Britain Today* (Milton Keynes: Open University Press, 1986).
5. C. Hakim, 'New Recruits to Self-employment in the 1980s', *Employment Gazette,* 97:6 (June 1989).
6. H. Bradley, *Men's Work, Women's Work* (Cambridge: Polity Press, 1989).
7. J. McColl, *The Value of the Awareness Campaign as a Tool for Stimulating Enterprise Amongst Women,* unpublished M.Sc. thesis (University of Stirling, 1989).
8. T. Cannon, S. Carter, P. Rosa, L. Baddon and R. McClure, *Female Entrepreneurs,* Report to the Department of Employment and Shell UK Ltd (University of Stirling: Scottish Enterprise Foundation, 1988).
9. Shiu-Ying L. Chan, *A Strategic Analysis of Current Support Provision for Female Entrepreneurs in Scotland,* unpublished M.Sc. thesis (University of Stirling, 1988).
10. C. Shakeshaft and M. Hanson, 'Androcentric Bias in the *Educational Administration Quarterly', Educational Administration Quarterly,* 22:1 (1986).
11. G. Koper, *Women Entrepreneurs and Business Credit Granting: Constraints and Possibilities,* paper presented to 'Women Entrepreneurs' conference (University of Bradford, 1989).
12. Cannon et al., op. cit.
13. The details of the campaign are presented in C. Hartshorn and R.McClure, 'Unlocking Enterprise: The Entrepreneurial Potential of Scottish Women' (University of Stirling: Scottish Enterprise Foundation, 1990).
14. Kotler and Roberto, op. cit.
15. McColl, op. cit.
16. Kotler and Roberto, op. cit., p. 225.
17. Cannon et al., op. cit.

18. J. Curran and R. Burrows, 'National Profiles of the Self-employed', *Employment Gazette*, 97:7 (July 1989).

19. R. Goffee and R. Scase, *Women in Charge: The Experience of Female Entrepreneurs* (London: Allen and Unwin, 1985).

20. R. D. Hisrich and C. Brush, 'The Woman Entrepreneur: Implications of Family, Education and Occupational Experience, in *Frontiers of Entrepreneurship Research* (MA: Babson Center for Entrepreneurial Studies, 1983), pp. 255–70.

21. Hakin (1989), op. cit.

22. Cannon et al., op. cit.

23. J. Curran and Stanworth, 'Education and Training for Enterprise: Some Problems of Classification, Evaluation, Policy and Research, *International Small Business Journal*, 7:2 (1989).

24. P. Lazarsfeld and R. Merton, 'Mass Communication, Popular Taste, and Organised Social Action', in William Schramm (ed.), *Mass Communications* (Urbana: University of Illinois Press, 1949).

25. G. D. Wiebe, 'Merchandising Commodities and Citizenship on Television', *Public Opinion Quarterly*, 15 (Winter 1951–2).

26. Lazarsfeld and Merton, op. cit.

Chapter 5

———————◆———————

WOMEN'S EDUCATION AND TRAINING, AND EMPLOYMENT BARRIERS AFFECTING WOMEN IN SWAZILAND

Nomcebo O. Simelane and Nonhlanhla F. Dlamini

Lack of education is one factor that militates against the rights and welfare of women in Swaziland. Most African governments have become aware that education is probably the most important medium through which individuals can express themselves. Therefore, Swaziland's policy is to provide free and equal educational opportunities to all its citizens. In this regard, one of the principles that has been advanced as underlying educational development in Swaziland is that education is the 'inalienable right' of every Swazi citizen, and therefore the state's duty is to ensure that all Swazis are assisted to have access to education.

Over the years, the government's policy has been and continues to be 'universal primary education'. Government in this context pledges commitment to providing primary education to all children of school-going age in the kingdom. This goal has not yet been achieved, even though great strides have been made in that direction. However, government's policy of affording opportunities for every citizen in Swaziland is a theory which has been found to be very different from practice. There are still traces of inequalities between the sexes in the attainment of education.

The population census of 1986 apparently indicates that girls have better chances to attend school than boys have. A lower proportion of girls than boys is found in school at lower primary age (i.e. between the ages of 5 and 9), and a lower proportion of girls than boys from all ages between 5 and 19 has never been to school (see Table 5.1). However, although the picture is presented thus, interestingly enough the school enrolment shows that there are more boys than girls (see Table 5.2), and even future projections show that this trend is likely to continue.

Several reasons have been advanced to explain this. One is that many girls fall pregnant and must drop out of school, as the suspension of a pregnant student is required by education rules. Another is that parents favour boys because they feel that girls will either fall pregnant or marry and leave their families, whereas a

TABLE 5.1:   School attendance pattern, by age and sex, as percentages, 1986.

Age group	Attending full-time male	Attending full-time female	Attended previously male	Attended previously female	Never attended male	Never attended female
5–9	44.8	48.8	1.0	1.1	53.0	50.0
10–19	69.6	64.8	15.8	23.0	14.0	11.8
20–29	8.3	3.6	70.6	73.6	20.0	22.0

Source:1986 Census, Vol. 1, Table 7.1.

TABLE 5.2:   Primary school enrolment, by year and sex, 1986–96.

Year	Boys	Girls	Total	% Growth
1986	7145	70731	142206	–
1987	74215	73528	147743	3.89
1988	76815	76080	152895	3.49
1989	78835	78510	157345	5.79
1990	83788	83666	166454	5.56
1991	87246	85662	172908	3.98
1992	89021	87227	176248	–
1993	91689	89671	181359	–
1994	94438	92180	186618	–
1995	97272	94758	192030	–
1996	100192	97407	197599	–

Source: Ministry of Education Statistics,1992.

boy remains part of the family even when married. Another reason why fewer girls receive education is that girls leave the school system voluntarily because they have more job opportunities for work requiring little education, such as being domestic servants or seasonal workers.

Again, upon examination of the attendance patterns in school, for the age group between 10 and 19, a higher proportion of boys is in school than girls. A quarter of all girls have already left school, compared to only 15.8 per cent of boys. This pattern continues for those over 20, and it is rare for girls over 20 to be at school (see Table 5.1). Two explanations have been offered for this pattern: late entry of boys to school because of work at home, particularly cattle-herding, and the unequal pressure on boys as potential earners to acquire educational qualifications. Yet another reason could be identified, namely that girls tend to complete their education earlier because of their superior educational attainment to boys.

On examination of the attainment of those aged between 20 and 24, the picture of superior female attainment disappears. Males of this age are disproportionately represented at university, where, despite their smaller numbers in the population, they outnumber girls (see Table 5.3). At university, their performance exceeds that of girls. Fewer girls also sit post-school vocational diplomas (see Table 5.4).

TABLE 5.3: University Student Enrolment by Gender 1987–92.

	1987–8	1988–9	1989–0	1990–1	1991–2	1992–3
Male	833	879	931	965	961	956
Female	575	620	670	754	744	770
Total	1408	1499	1601	1716	170	1726

Source: Ministry of Education Statistics, 1992.

TABLE 5.4: Enrolment in technical and artisan training, by sex, 1987–92.

Gender	1987–8	1988–9	1989–90	1990–1	1991–2
Male	390	864	–	769	772
Female	193	209	–	204	339
Total	583	1073	0	973	1111

Source: Ministry of Education Statistics, 1992.

Society has also reserved *certain fields* and subjects of education for men, in that there exist typically 'male' jobs. Women, right from young ages, are discouraged from venturing into these fields. For instance, secondary-school subject choices of girls differ from boys, with a marked avoidance by girls of maths and sciences. Research shows that girls are not incompetent as science scholars, but they receive no encouragement, since many scientific careers are seen as 'not readily accessible to women'. In another area, boys traditionally take technical subjects while girls take home economics and agriculture. The division is said to be less rigid, although selection of subjects is still gender-driven to some extent. The differentiation in subject selection is being bridged as girls are now taking technical studies and boys are also taking home economics. The intention is that, over time, school subjects will become less gender-stereotyped in Swaziland.

The level of education for women and the attitude of stereotyping certain fields of study as reserved for males has also had an impact on the trend of careers in which women are concentrated. Women are predominantly in the nursing and teaching occupations, while men, on the other hand, dominate the fewer, better-paid administrative and managerial positions. For instance, in 1991, there were 5,347 primary teachers in the country, with women accounting for 4,157 (77 per cent) of this number.

In conclusion, there is a direct relationship between the level of education and skill-acquisition and employment and career opportunities in the formal sector. Girls receive less education than boys for a number of reasons, some of which include: teenage pregnancies; the insecurity for parents in educating a girl who is, after all, expected to move out of her family to her husband's family; and abundant job opportunities as domestic or manual and seasonal workers which require fewer, if any, qualifications. Financial investment in the education of a girl is seen as a waste of money, and consequently the enrolment rates of girls as opposed to boys decrease from secondary school to post-high-school training.

Again, looking at women's educational attainment in the higher institutions of learning, a gap between males and females is witnessed, with males dominating. There is still the tendency for females to be concentrated in the lower-paying, lower-status professions, such as nursing and teaching.

The Rights of Women in the Workplace

In Swaziland, women comprise over half of the total population. They perform important economic, social and cultural functions which can no longer be ignored or considered marginal in the realities of Swaziland's development in terms of their roles in the society and their importance as potential human resources.

Despite their contribution as farmers, traders, teachers and caretakers of families, women largely have no access to the means of production, knowledge and skills which would facilitate the upgrading and further utilisation of their potential in the development efforts. Women in Swaziland experience some inequality before the law in regard to their position at work, and as a result cannot contribute fully to the development of their country. The absence of adequate data regarding the economic value of their roles has continued to contribute to the underestimation of their work, leading to an almost total neglect of their needs in national development plans.

In Swaziland, the population is employed in the formal sector (which covers both the private and the public sectors) and by the informal sector (which is self-employment). The latter sector is where most Swazi women are employed, and they acquire cash incomes by 'such homestead-based activities as medicine, and selling handicraft'. Out of necessity, not by choice, women work and take jobs in the formal sector for the same reasons as men, that is, either to supplement the family income or to support their children, and also to give themselves a valuable sense of independence. However, outstanding inequalities between the sexes in employment are experienced, and there are also legal constraints that serve to deter women in Swaziland from participating fully in the economic development of the country. In several areas, legal impediments have been identified as inhibiting women from participating fully in the employment arena.

Women's Status: A Synthesis
Swazi society, like any other society, operates within the framework of existing laws and regulations that control the degree of freedom and participation in the activities of the society. The degree of participation of women in Swaziland is very limited due to legal restrictions that relegate women, especially married women, to minor status. Whatever steps are taken to increase their participation in any field of work, women's achievements will remain very low and limited if some policy issues are not resolved. It is true that laws which inhibit women's involvement are a prolongation of the traditional attitudes towards women. But in a modern society with the intricacies of modern development issues, their existence is no longer valid, not only for the sake of social

justice but also more for economic growth, self-reliance and stability, which are national goals for development.

Acknowledgements

This chapter is extracted from a study commissioned by the International Planned Parenthood Federation, Africa Region, 1995, entitled 'Legal and Policy Barriers Affecting Delivery of Family Planning Services in Swaziland', with kind permission from the authors. Thanks are due to Mrs M. Khoza, Principal of the Swaziland Institute of Management and Public Administration, for her assistance with this. A summary of this document was circulated as part of the United Nations Fourth World Conference on Women, held in Beijing, China, in September 1995.

Part 3

Women's Access to Jobs and Skills

Chapter 6

 ◆

Overcoming the Barriers

Angela O'Hagan

The Role of the Equal Opportunities Commission
The Equal Opportunities Commission (EOC) has a support and advisory role in the UK, working to progress good practice in equal opportunities, by preventing discrimination and encouraging greater recognition of the benefits of non-discriminatory practice. In this regard, the EOC works mainly with employers and equal-opportunities or personnel practitioners, but also with trades unions, voluntary orientations and policy bodies.

The EOC is increasingly working towards a position of greater influence and consultation with the policy community in Scotland, namely the various government departments and national economic policy and development agencies. The EOC is involved in a range of activities designed to improve the integration of equalities issues in policymaking in Scotland.

The Barriers: A Picture of Scotland
In addressing this theme of 'Women's Access to Jobs and Skills', we must first ask where women are in the labour market in Scotland. The short answer is that they are not in the boardrooms and inner cabinets of corporate or political interests. Of the top 150 company directors in Scotland, three are women, and they are non-executive directors.

Job Segregation

In Scotland, part-time workers account for over 40 per cent of women in work, while over 75 per cent of all part-time workers are women.[1] Women continue to be concentrated in certain occupational areas in Scotland, and indeed throughout the UK. In Scotland, women comprise 77 per cent of clerical and secretarial workers, 66 per cent of sales staff, 65 per cent of public administration workers, 59 per cent of distribution, catering and hospitality workers, and 46.6 per cent of banking and finance-sector workers. The foregoing is the breakdown of the occupations of 52 per cent of the total population of Scotland, of whom 52 per cent are economically active, while there is 7 per cent unemployment among women in Scotland. Statistics for employed status in the UK include people on government-sponsored training schemes and unpaid family workers.

Childcare

Lack of access to affordable childcare, lack of information on available childcare and lack of provision overall have consistently been identified as being among the main barriers to women's participation in economic life, that is, to the labour market. Women with children face greater barriers to employment than single women or women without children, such as those women advancing in management and the professions. The economically active population includes 65 per cent of women with dependent children and 73 per cent of those without children.

Employment Opportunities

In the EOC's *Equality Issues in Scotland: A Research Review,*[2] lack of suitable employment opportunities was identified as another barrier to women's access to jobs and skills. There are a number of contributory factors to this:

- social pressures and attitudes to what constitutes 'women's work'. Recent research has highlighted that in Scotland there continue to be negative, even hostile, attitudes to women's participation in employment and training.
- absence of childcare, of care for dependants, and of flexible working opportunities.
- lack of labour-market information and access for women who are not currently in the labour market or participating in training opportunities.
- men in employment have greater access to skills training and to vocational and occupational training than women.
- employers' practices include barriers to women in the recruitment and selection process, and discriminatory attitudes and procedures.

Educational Opportunities

Women in Scotland are higher educational achievers than men. In secondary schools in Scotland, girls' performances have been increasing over the last few years, but nevertheless this performance continues to be in segregated subjects. Girls continue to be in the majority in English, foreign languages, the 'softer sciences' and business studies.

In higher education, there are more women full-time students. Women can surmount the subject-segregation barriers into medical and science-related occupations: over 50 per cent of medicine and dentistry students are women. But in management occupations, that figure is reversed in the 'hard sciences' of physics and mathematics, where well over 50 per cent of these students are men.

This gap in educational achievement and representation in employment is even more pronounced for black and minority ethnic women. In Scotland, the highest educational achievers are black or Afro-Caribbean women, with Chinese women coming second. In employment, black and minority ethnic women face the double discrimination of sex and race discrimination.

Pay

Inequalities in pay are where the most pronounced discrimination is manifest. In Scotland, women earn only 80 per cent of men's wages on average, while this gap is even greater for black and ethnic minority women. In 1992, research showed that these women earned up to 23 per cent less than white women. In Scotland, there is more pronounced inequality across the regions: in the north-east, women earn up to 40 per cent less than men, and in areas of industrial decline or in rural economies the gap is around 30 per cent.

Obviously, this pay gap has implications for women's access to jobs and skills. Concentrating women in low-paid and lower-status jobs impacts upon their ability to find affordable childcare, and consequently reduces opportunities for further training for promotion in employment. In EOC research of 1994, it was identified that one-third of British women workers are low-paid.[3] Of the 2.6 million workers who earn less than the National Insurance lower earnings limit of £57 per week, 2.3 million were women. This research identified certain characteristics of women in low pay:

- few educational qualifications
- part-time working in semi-skilled or unskilled occupations
- limited experience of full-time work
- caring responsibilities
- have received little training
- are part of low-income households
- work in smaller private-sector companies, without trade-union membership.

Future Projections

In looking towards the year 2000, research again has highlighted the following prospects for women:[4]

- reliance on male incomes, which remains the principal source of income for most households. The poorest people in society are women

- future employment prospects: male unemployment is increasing; full-time job opportunities are decreasing. It is anticipated that the labour force will grow by some 500,000 while the male labour force will decline in almost similar proportions. Although there will be more employment opportunities, they will be part-time and in lower-skilled areas.

So, access to training and education will become even more essential if women are to escape this structure. The job opportunities will be in the growth of the service sector. Where women will again lose ground is in the middle employment areas of clerical and administrative occupations, where they currently predominate. A scenario is envisaged where employment opportunities for women will be for highly-qualified women in management and professional posts, or at the other extreme of low-paid, low-status jobs.

One possibly positive projection is that women will increase in representation as managers, professionals and associated professionals, to 38 per cent, 41 per cent and 58 per cent respectively. The downside of this is the potential for a greater divide between women, as well as between men and women.

In highlighting where discrimination occurs, job segregation again is the cause of discrimination between women and women, as well as men and women. Looking at pay differentials of men and women in employment, a picture emerges of women in segregated occupations, men in management positions, and pay levels across those occupations diverging, with a lack of consistency and an unequal calculation basis. This pay gap exists despite twenty years of equal-pay legislation.

The foregoing is a sample of the national trends and forecasts. The EOC is concerned to work with employers, not just to ensure that the legislation is adhered to, but also to move towards greater integration of equal-opportunities policies and practices in employment as a fundamental element of business practice.

Current Issues
Recruitment and Selection

Recruitment and selection continues to be a major area of discrimination and an additional barrier to women's participation in the labour market, despite the Sex Discrimination Act. The majority of complaints which the EOC receives through the officer in Scotland are concerned with discrimination at the point of selection. Many of these complaints are still related to pregnancy and maternity. Much of the work that is undertaken with employers involves training on equal-opportunities policy development and implementation of equality-'proofed' recruitment and selection procedures. A considerable amount of time is still addressed to issues of job descriptions and person specifications, application forms and monitoring procedures.

Employment Structures

As is the trend all over the UK, in Scotland we are experiencing the effects of an increasingly deregulated employment market. Employment structures are fragmenting, for men as well as women. Increasingly, we are witnessing practices of temporary contracts, part-time working and, worse still, key worker and zero-hours contracts. Under these latter arrangements, individuals are uncertain as to the hours they will be working in a given week;

many will work without a written contract of employment, and will work up to just below the threshold of sixteen hours per week which gives them access to fuller employment rights.

Upon examining the economic effects of these employment practices and the detrimental effect on local and national economies that the exclusion of women from full employment opportunities represents,[5] it is clear that there is a cost to the national Exchequer, and directly to local economies and indeed families.

We are now in an environment where more and more households have multiple income sources to maintain any standard of living, or indeed to meet ordinary living costs. Fewer women with children, especially young mothers, are working: in twenty years since 1973, there has been a fall of 20 per cent of young mothers working. Part of this problem is the benefits system and changes to the social-security system which act as a barrier to women taking up paid employment. This takes us back to the core problem of access to childcare.

Local Government Reform
In Scotland, we are currently undergoing a process of reorganisation of the structure of local government, reducing sixty-five regional, district and island authorities to a total of twenty-nine 'unitary' authorities. This reform has considerable implications for equality of opportunity and for women's employment. In 1995 some 300,000 women were employed in local authorities in Scotland, again concentrated in administrative and clerical roles, with only 20 per cent of women in local government at Principal Officer level or above. There are no women Chief Executives in Scottish local government.

This reform also has obvious implications for women's employment opportunities, and the potential for sex discrimination is of real concern to the EOC. We have taken steps to raise awareness of this potential for discrimination, but also to highlight the good practice that has been developed by local authorities in Scotland. Local authorities are not only employers of large numbers of women, but they are also role models, or touchstones for employment practices in other sectors. They can obviously have influence on the wider community and the employment community. Safeguarding good employment practice is, we would argue, a fundamental duty for local authorities, and indeed for all employers.

This recent restructuring is part of a series of reforms in local-authority operations. The introduction of the Compulsory Competitive Tendering Systems, where core local-authority responsibilities must be open to a competitive process, and the practice of contracts being awarded on price have had a considerable negative impact on women's employment opportunities, standards of terms and conditions, and wage levels. In a recent EOC survey, it was found that women had suffered 96 per cent of the job losses through this process.[6] The areas of cleaning and catering, where women are predominantly employed, have seen reductions in wage levels and in hours of work. In short, this has resulted in 25 per cent of women in these jobs working to several contracts, within the same authority, with some failing to reach the sixteen hours per week which would bring them employment rights; and some are even failing to earn the National Insurance Lower Earnings Limit of £57 per week.

In all, the process of local government reform will impact upon employment and services-delivery policies and practices which have been developed within an equality framework. There are also implications for women's employment, local-authority involvement in training and employment-creation projects, access to job and skill opportunities, for example, transport, childcare, and access to related facilities.

80

Vocational Training

The EOC has some concerns regarding the current structure of government-sponsored training, and is currently consulting across all education and training sectors on a strategy for equal opportunities in training and education in Scotland. This strategy addresses the issues of employment segregation and indirect discrimination that are so apparent in employment in education. It looks at curricular content and non-stereotyped education for all ages, and addresses issues of careers advice and vocational training.

Where prejudices or inherent discriminatory attitudes exist, the result is often to channel men and women into 'traditional' roles. We have some concerns that the government-sponsored training programmes and those responsible for their implementation, at either policy or delivery level, may perpetuate this stereotyping. For example, the unit costs of some vocational qualifications are higher than others, and tend to be in the traditionally male-dominated areas of engineering and technology. Women still predominate in the equally traditional areas of business administration and, for example, hairdressing, which have lower rates of pay and lower rates of unit costs for training provision.

Monitoring this area of government policy and funding is crucial if the potential for discrimination is to be eliminated from the process. We have urged the Local Enterprise Company network to improve and increase the volume of statistics produced on the take-up of training opportunities and to provide more information on the gender breakdown of training places in occupational and skills areas, and on the outcomes from those training opportunities.

The Way Forward
Working with Employers
In trying to overcome the barriers and remove the prejudices to

women's access to jobs and skills, we can employ the arguments of equity, justice and fairness. It is increasingly my experience, which has been borne out by the research since the early 1980s, that whatever one's personal convictions are, the arguments which one has to use are those related to organisational effectiveness and benefit to business. There are many benefits to business and to the effectiveness of an organisation if it does not discriminate against 50 per cent of the population and all the skills, expertise and experience that these individuals represent. Since this seems a rather straightforward argument, it remains a mystery why some people have so much difficulty with it.

The work of organisations like Opportunity 2000 in conjunction with the Institute of Personnel Management (as it was then called) in calculating the cost to business of poor employment practices and discrimination where women were not encouraged to return to employment after maternity-related breaks, for example, has been tremendously helpful in advancing the debate on the contribution of women's employment. Equally, repeated research evidence indicates the projected change in women's behaviour in the labour market if certain barriers to participation were removed: more women would work.

There are obvious benefits to the local economy of more women in work, but there are huge potential returns to the Treasury in the payments of NI and tax contributions by women working. So, those of us involved in presenting these arguments must concentrate on encouraging employers to recognising the value of women's contribution to the overall economy and the individual bottom-line considerations:

- women are capable of succeeding in far more than the lower-status, segregated areas in which they find themselves

- women can bring additional skills and experience to employment
- women's educational achievements are worth harnessing
- greater organisational effectiveness can come from greater diversity of the organisation; adherence to 'sameness' can make an organisation less effective.

We must promote the arguments in favour of women's inclusion and full participation in the labour market:

- local economic and national economic return
- less reliance on the social-security benefits system
- greater contribution to skills and competitiveness development.

Finally, there are the arguments concerning the cost of discrimination. It is not the most positive or developmental approach to remind employers of the punitive response that may await their discriminatory behaviour. Nevertheless, the EOC is a law-enforcement agency, and the law exists to protect individuals and to provide them with a remedy for injustice suffered. Therefore, the EOC reminds employers that there is now no limit on the level of compensation that can be awarded in Industrial Tribunal decisions, and that their corporate energies would be better directed towards preventing discrimination in the first place, rather than trying to prove that they did not discriminate.

For a national utility company to allow itself to lose an Industrial Tribunal decision in February 1995, which found that the company could not objectively justify refusing to allow job-sharing – when it had a policy! – is not only discrimination but is also very poor management and business practice. The actions of one group of management and a series of negative decisions have cost that company £35,000 in compensation. That award is in addition to the loss of the experience and competence of a Team Leader who had been with the company for seventeen years, as well as the investment which she represented for the company in terms of training, direct staff costs and so forth. All that training and experience has now gone to benefit another company.

Increased Awareness and Understanding

There is a role for all representatives of statutory agencies, government or public bodies, advisory agencies and employers – whatever the size – to increase understanding of what constitutes discrimination, of the negative consequences which it has for everyone, and of the collective responsibility to prevent it from occurring in the first place.

For individuals and employers, greater knowledge of the legislative framework is one important area of awareness-raising. Individual women's level of knowledge of their rights is very low; they may know that direct discrimination is unlawful, but they may only feel that unequal pay is not fair rather than unlawful. The legal framework is extremely complicated for anyone, and certainly for a woman marginalised because of her economic circumstances. Therefore, the statutory agencies such as the EOC and related advocacy agencies have a responsibility to continue to disseminate information on individuals' rights through a variety of media and by accessing a range of resources.

For employers, the legal framework is also very complicated and changing rapidly. It is not easy to keep abreast of and understand the many twists and turns of discrimination and employment law and decisions from Europe. However, one's sympathies run out when one witnesses employers who direct no interest, far less resources, towards accessing the information that they need. Not only are these employers ignoring their legal responsibilities, but they are also blind to the wider organisational benefits that non-discriminatory practice offers their company.

The EOC tries to meet these information needs in various ways. One of its potentially most powerful tools is 'The Equality Exchange', a membership service for employers which provides them with up-to-date information on the legal position, but also on developments in good practice. It is a forum for employers to come together to share experience and information on common issues and to learn from one another's experience and practice.

In this way, a whole range of employers learn about the practicalities of good practice in employment, but they also learn that if such large companies as British Gas, the Royal Mail and British Telecom think it is a worthwhile exercise to have (for example) a comprehensive policy on sexual harassment, supported by practical procedures, a training programme and a counselling network, then it is to be hoped that they will take appropriate action in their own organisations to follow this lead.

Ensuring that we all keep up to date on trends in good practice is not easy. In many ways, although I am closely involved in the Equality Exchange, a large proportion of the other enquiries which I receive are from individuals who are reporting bad practice or trying to improve on practice in their organisation. Fortunately, there are far more people in the latter category than the former.

The main users of the Exchange are human-resource practitioners, equal-opportunity managers and so forth. The benefits which they find from the Exchange are ones of information and support.

Training

With regard to national and strategic training programmes, the EOC gave evidence to the 1994 Scottish Affairs Committee on the operation of Scottish Enterprise (SE), Highlands and Islands Enterprise (HIE) and the Local Enterprise Companies (LECs)

Network. In common with many policy recommendations from the EOC, we argued for greater flexibility in the approach to training delivery and opportunities. The demand for flexibility has been echoed by the LEC network and indeed by employers. Although the reasons behind these representations do vary slightly, there is commonality of approach in aiming for more effectively-targeted skills training opportunities for all.

In order to make more informed decisions with greater strategic focus, information on the take-up and outcomes of training opportunities is vital. Providing a gender breakdown of these statistics is essential to identify the potential for effective positive action programmes and to address current or future skills gaps and make provision according to local and employer need. Although training through the LECs only accounts for a small proportion of the overall expenditure on training (in 1993, private-sector companies spent over £2 billion on training, while the budget through SE and HIE was £170 million and £12.5 million respectively), the training provided through the LEC network is largely access training and vocational training, not for people already in work but rather to improve access to employment opportunities.

The Select Committee responded positively to the EOC's recommendations and to those from other agencies across the spectrum of equalities issues, as well as those from employer and business interests.

- Greater flexibility and transparency were the key recommendations in this regard. Employers should make opportunities more accessible and should publicise activities to inform themselves, others and the public of the success of their efforts.
- Allowances should be made for greater needs-driven provision (e.g. part-time training, localised delivery,

publication of results) while ensuring that the principles of equal opportunities are adhered to and are regarded as an integral business function and contractual responsibility for the LECs as quasi-governmental organisations.

The Fair Play Consortium Scotland

A partnership or collective approach is the way that the EOC has found to be most effective in reaching our audience, whether that audience is women from urban housing estates or directors in local government: accessing common channels of communication and sources of information makes effective use of resources and effective promotion of key messages.

These are the arguments which I very often use with employers, or when working with personnel or human-resource practitioners within organisations. Make use of the resources that are already available, thereby not allowing the key issues of women's representation and greater opportunity to be sidetracked into a resource argument. Ensure that any systems set up around equal-opportunities monitoring, for example, or other procedures, provide for other management information uses as well, such as training-needs analyses. In this way, by ensuring that equal-opportunities systems are installed and functioning, there is greater likelihood that the objective of making equal-opportunities practice integral to the organisation will be achieved.

The Fair Play Consortium for Scotland is a new initiative, launched in 1996, which follows the examples of similar initiatives in Wales, and later in England, where the policy and employment communities are brought together to address the issues of women's access to jobs and skills. The EOC aims through this new initiative, to work with other organisations towards a better understanding of the barriers among policymakers and decision-makers, and ultimately to a situation where these issues form an integral part of the policymaking process. In this way, what we hope to achieve is a situation where equal-opportunities issues are not viewed as separate and alien from economic development policies and strategies. This means that childcare initiatives (and problems), for example, are not an add-on afterthought feature of an employment programme, but that childcare is in itself an employment programme, so that any other employment-generation projects will have identified and addressed the core issues of childcare from the outset.

In brief, the following is the EOC's way forward in Scotland:

- encouraging partnerships;
- seeking opportunities for joint working;
- formulating a strategic approach to the range of issues affecting women's access to jobs and skills;
- reinforcing the fact that the arguments relating to women's participation in employment are inextricably linked to economic and social development.

Notes

1. Unless otherwise stated, the statistics in this chapter have been adapted from: Equal Opportunities Commission, *Facts about Women and Men in Scotland 1994* (EOC, 1994).
2. Equal Opportunities Commission, *Equality Issues in Scotland: A Research Review* (EOC, 1994).
3. S. Dex, S. Lissenburgh and M. Taylor, *Women and Low Pay: Identifying the Issues* (EOC, 1994).
4. Equal Opportunities Commission, *The Economics of Equal Opportunities* (EOC, 1995).
5. Ibid.
6. Equal Opportunities Commission, *Quality through Equality: Good Practice in Equal Opportunities in Scottish Local Authorities* (EOC, 1995).

Chapter 7

◆

THE SITUATION OF WOMEN IN POLAND
REPORT FOR THE UNITED NATIONS FOURTH WORLD CONFERENCE ON WOMEN, BEIJING, CHINA, SEPTEMBER 1995

Maria Anna Knothe, Ewa Lizowska and Elzbieta Wlodyka

Unemployment among Women

The political and economic system in force in Poland up to 1989 by definition created full employment for all people prepared to work. Unemployment was considered an ideological symbol of the enemy capitalist system. From the moment the economic transformation in Poland began, however, it was not so much ideology as production costs, mismatch of the employers' needs and the workers' qualifications, in short all the ingredients of a market economy, that turned out to be the culprits of the massive unemployment that followed.

In 1994, the level of unemployment showed nil growth for the first time in five years. This is no cause for satisfaction, as it is only a symptom of stagnation, while statistics show that at the beginning of 1995 there were 2.8 million registered unemployed (16.6 per cent of the workforce), of whom 1.5 million were women. This makes women the majority (54 per cent) of registered unemployed,[1] but this is not the full story. The experience of the employment agency attached to the Centre for the Advancement of Women (a non-government organisation) suggests that fully half of all women seeking work have not troubled to register in a government employment office. It can be safely inferred that the real number of job-seekers far exceeds the official figures.

Unemployment affects a wide range of geographic, social and demographic categories. The Slupsk voivodship has the highest unemployment level, at 35 per cent, while Warsaw and the surrounding conurbation have the lowest, at 6.3 per cent. Job-market changes and unemployment affect women far more than men. The number of women in jobs is steadily falling, from 78 per cent in 1985 to 71 per cent in 1990, and 57 per cent in 1994 (women make up 45 per cent of the total workforce).

The number of women in state-sector jobs is also decreasing. Mass layoffs mainly affect women, who are also more vulnerable to long-term unemployment[2] because there are fewer job vacancies for them and employers demand more of women. Young school-leavers are hardest hit; unemployment for women aged 15–19 living in towns is nearly 53 per cent (48 per cent for young men in the same age group). Recent years have also seen more women aged 35–44 losing their jobs.[3] This is the most professionally productive time for women, as their domestic duties are declining. Nor is education any longer a hedge against unemployment: 'Women with general secondary and vocational education together make up 37.8 per cent of unemployed women (May 1993 figures) whilst the equivalent figure for men is 19.1 per cent'.[4] Highly-qualified men generally do better on the job market than equally-qualified women.

Discrimination against Women in the Job Market
The reason for this difficult job-market situation for women is blatant discrimination against women. This is supported by the results of a study entitled 'The Warsaw Job Market of Women', initiated by the Centre for the Advancement of Women in May–June 1993. The study embraced 407 employers in both the

state and the private sector. The main object was to find answers to the questions: 'What kind of workers are today's employers seeking?'; 'What qualifications are most in demand?'; 'What personal attributes are decisive in landing a job?' It was hoped that the results of the study would give some useful pointers to the direction that retraining should take and what subjects it should cover to increase women's chances of getting jobs. The results are highly interesting, and some of the findings are as follows.

- Men obtain twice as many new jobs as women. There is even growing interest in giving men jobs traditionally the preserve of women, for example in retail and service industries.
- As well as this easing of women out of retail and service industries, there is now declining interest in employing women in jobs requiring high office administration skills and qualifications.
- Women hold far fewer management positions than men; this is more often true of the private sector than the state sector.
- The group most at risk of layoffs are women aged 40 and over in state-sector office jobs; this group is the dominant clientele of employment agencies. Not only do they have the most difficulty finding another job, but it is also extremely hard to persuade them to retrain and qualify for something else because of age-related psychological barriers.
- Analysis of questions put to job candidates reveals that 'discrimination against women on the Warsaw job market is evident'.[5] This discrimination stems on the one hand from traditional thought patterns about a woman's role; it is 'natural' for her to be at home, nurturing and raising children as well as accepting responsibility for procreation.

91

On the other hand, legislation dating back to the 1960s prescribing privileges for working women to make their double role easier has begun to work against them in recent years in the competitive job market. From an employer's point of view, women are less attractive as employees because they have to be granted certain assurances that do not apply to men.

TABLE 7.1: Gainfully employed persons by level of education (per cent).

Level of education	Women	Men
Higher	10	9
Post-college	5	1
Vocational college	24	21
General college	11	3
Secondary vocational	24	41
Secondary general	26	24

Source: based on Central Statistical Office data, 1994.

Half the women with jobs in 1993 were educated to at least college level, whereas the equivalent figure for men was only 34 per cent (see Table 7.1). It can be inferred from this that women are better educated than men, yet they suffer higher unemployment. It is also evidence of discrimination against women on the job market. Another relevant factor is the fact that, in today's conditions, formal education counts for much less than specific skills, high work motivation, energy, creativity and responsibility, qualities which were not especially nurtured in the previous system.

Women Entrepreneurs

Increasingly, women start their own businesses as a means of satisfying their need for personal development, creativity and independence in decision-making, as well as a higher income.

Women starting their own firms are a new and dynamic phenomenon in this part of Europe; in Poland, the number of women entrepreneurs rose from 3.7 per cent of the total female workforce in 1989 to 7.5 per cent in 1991 and about 11 per cent in 1993, and of those the number who owned their businesses were 27 per cent in 1989, 33 per cent in 1991 and approximately 39 per cent in 1993.[6]

Setting up in business is one of the ways of combating unemployment, especially for college-educated women aged 40 or over. The few studies on women business owners conducted to date show that it is mainly college- and higher-educated women who start their own firms. About half of women entrepreneurs are aged 40–9.

One of the main barriers to women setting up in business seems to be the stereotype that mothering and housekeeping are the only roles that women are good at. In fact, women as a population represent a wide cross-section; there are those who derive full satisfaction from running their home and raising children, but at the other end of the scale there are also those who need more than their family to feel fulfilled and satisfied. And for those active and enterprising women, setting up in business is a way to achieve that fulfilment. It is in everyone's interest to give such women the support they need, and to help to create conditions that allow them to thrive, thus stimulating the economy and reducing unemployment. There is a need for local programmes to support women's small businesses. These would help find information about business development finance and would provide free or inexpensive education on setting up and running a small business. Some women's organisations (for example, the Centre for the Advancement of Women, the International Forum for Women in Warsaw, and the International Foundation of Women in Łódź) do run such programmes but they are limited in both scale and scope. There are still too few such programmes; many more are needed. Women need to be strengthened in the belief that they can do a lot for themselves.

The results of a December 1994 survey of women business proprietors[7] point to the following conclusions.

1. The circumstances of women setting up in business vary greatly from individual to individual. Significant factors were the set of values from the parental home (important or very important for 54 per cent of respondents), and experience gained in workplaces with a social dimension (important for 61 per cent). There were also psychological factors: a desire for independence (91 per cent of respondents) and innate enterprise (81 per cent). But the most important and motivating factor by far was reasonable remuneration, cited by 94 per cent of respondents. Fear of unemployment was mentioned by 28 per cent of the women.

2. Women running their own firms experienced a great many insufficiencies. Most often, it was uncertainty of the tax regulations (81 per cent of women), no time for rest and recreation (78 per cent), for private life (71 per cent) or for family (68 per cent). Lack of money for business growth was reported by 55 per cent of women business proprietors, lack of legal knowledge by 57 per cent, and lack of economic knowledge by 34 per cent. About 60 per cent of the women felt keenly disadvantaged by market competition and difficulty finding customers, also by the rawness of Polish capitalism (unprincipled behaviour, dishonest dealings). Women generally start their businesses cautiously, broadening the scope and inventory step by step. Nevertheless, businesses run by women are not confined to just the dominant clothing and footwear

industries, but also extend to such things as electrical goods manufacture, building materials and tools.

3. Most women business proprietors (69 per cent) do not consider that they are treated any differently from male entrepreneurs. Nevertheless, 18 per cent responded that 'it varies', while 7 per cent stated definitely that they are treated worse.

4. Single women more often than married women reported difficulties in starting (single, 63 per cent; married, 30 per cent) and running (69 per cent and 40 per cent) their own businesses, also more often reporting inferior treatment compared with male entrepreneurs. This would appear to stem from the dominant traditional stereotyped Polish attitudes towards a woman's role and place in society.

Conclusions

One of the greatest benefits of the system-transformation is the acknowledgement of the importance of a middle class and the removal of obstacles to the development of small and medium-sized businesses. Women have enormous potential here; the trading and servicing sector, which is still largely underdeveloped in Poland, is within their domain. We already have many examples of women who have done well, proving that the hardest thing is to believe in success and thus overcome the typical feminine psychological barriers.

The most prominent factor making it hard for women to go into business and run their own firms is the problem of reconciling domestic and business duties. The role conflict which undoubtedly exists can be mitigated by the availability of services and easy access to childcare facilities, also by partners joining in with the housework. Most women support the idea that the fairest and most functionally suited contemporary scene is the kind of family partnership model where they can go out to work, whether out of choice or financial necessity.

Recommendations
At a time of high unemployment such as we have in Poland at present, there is a need to stimulate the economy on the one hand, and to develop large-scale education and retraining programmes for the unemployed on the other. There is also a need for special women's training programmes geared to actual job-market demands.

Acknowledgements
This chapter is extracted with the kind permission of the Polish Committee of NGOs, ul. Lwowska 17 m.3, 00-660 Warszawa, Poland, with special thanks to Maria Anna Knothe, Centre for the Advancement of Women, Warszawa, Poland.

WOMEN AND EDUCATION

Elzbieta Kalinowska

Preservation of Gender Stereotypes during the Process of Socialisation
From the first years of their lives, Polish girls and boys are exposed to the process of socialisation, which differs according to their gender. Mothers who are bringing up their children copy the same

methods which were used towards them in the past. Very often, one can hear mothers' remarks concerning 'inappropriate' behaviour addressed to their 3- or 4-year-old children: 'don't cry, you are not a girl'; 'be a brave man'; 'don't get filthy and do not behave as a boy'; 'a girl has to be clean and polite'.

Primary education is the level of education at which, in a very special and effective way, children are made familiar with the place of women and men in society. Teachers, completely unaware of this fact, use manuals that propagate a patriarchal model of the family and the world. Both the pictures and the texts printed in the manuals strengthen in a child's consciousness behaviour 'appropriate' to their gender.

Activities such as setting the table, feeding hens, playing with dolls, pouring juice, drawing flowers and making dishes are associated with a girl. A boy makes a model of a plane, plays chess, is interested in spaceships, takes part in fishing, collects stamps. According to the manuals' texts, only boys go for holidays and experience different adventures. Even at the level of primary education, girls are taught to be responsible for men's appearance and are made to feel guilty when they do not meet expectations.

In the manuals, only boys have plans and perspectives: 'Peter said: When I'm grown up, I will become a poet ... and you will have to call me "Master" ... Krysia finished the conversation on poetry and started to set the table for dinner'. In the manuals, a woman is shown only as a mother and a housewife. It is the woman who does all household jobs of cleaning, cooking, serving meals, shopping, washing, sewing and making dishes ('my mother takes care of the whole household'). Only the woman plays nursery roles: she washes and feeds a baby, goes for a walk with the children, takes them to the doctor, takes care of a sick child, helps children with their homework, discusses their school problems with them.

Such a mother usually does not work, does not have any friends or acquaintances, has no interests and in fact does not take part in any life outside the house; her contacts with other people are limited only to meetings with relatives. The only knowledge which we have of her work is obtained from information like 'mum is on duty' or 'mum will come back from work and she will not be able to prepare dinner'. However, this extraneous activity is not deemed worthy of admiration or respect; the manuals leave no doubt that only the father's professional work is important or valued.

The mother is loved by her children ('My mum is the best of all'), and receives flowers and scrolls on Mother's Day. The mother is always mentioned with warmth and care: 'My mother is tired, but she is in a good mood'. In general, the mother is always very ordinary, and while she is good and loving she also controls and punishes as well as being permanently tired.

The father-figure looks more attractive, more holiday-like (in pictures, he always wears a tie). He talks about interesting events, is familiar with technical matters, reads a lot, meets friends, has a hobby and receives a lot of family attention. Although the father rests a lot (takes a nap, reads a newspaper), he is never tired.

If a grandmother appears in the manuals, she usually replaces the mother in many household tasks: she takes care of her grandchildren, tells fairy-tales and delivers reprimands.

It happens quite often that the manuals' woman (unlike the mother) works. But the professional career belongs to anonymous women whose family life remains unknown. These women are different from those shown in family roles. The woman usually represents feminised professions: she is a teacher, a doctor, a nurse, a saleslady.

The situations described in the manuals are artificial, and because of their uniformity they are indistinct. The image of family and woman is accordingly adjusted. Whoever she is and whatever roles she plays, she always remains the same: without personal aspirations, humble, overworked, taking care of home and family, tired, but smiling. She does not get irritated, does not rebel, does not complain. She meekly complies with her fate.[8]

Although the Convention of Elimination of All Forms of Discrimination against Women, signed by Poland, obliges the Polish government to liquidate stereotyped concepts of male and female roles through revising the content of manuals, nothing has been made in this area. In recent years, many new manuals have been introduced into curricula but without being controlled from the point of view of their compliance with the Convention.

Inequality of Educational Opportunity

Unequal educational opportunities for girls and boys can be seen at the high-school and higher levels of education. However, at the primary level of education we can notice the facts proving the lack of equality in education. Technical classes, different for boys and girls, block the awakening of technical interests and skills among girls and strengthen social stereotypes of the roles of men and women. There is a well-known case of the intervention of the Polish Feminist Association related to computer classes for boys and housekeeping classes for girls.

Girls have fewer opportunities to choose the profile of education at high-school level. Vocational schools, where a lot of girls were trained, have been liquidated (tailoring schools collapsed together with the textile industry), and some technical schools do not accept girls at all. As a result, more girls than boys go to colleges that do not train students for any particular profession. After graduation, many girls have to continue their education at university, postgraduate schools or other higher education institutions in order to enter a profession.

Women make up more than half of all students (51.4 per cent in 1991) who graduate from higher education institutions. But the majority study only subjects giving qualifications for starting work in poorly-paid, feminised professions such as teaching, scientific work or medicine. In 1990–1, the percentages of women students in the major subject areas were as follows: humanitarian science (75.5), education (69.5), medical studies (62.5), mathematics (60.3), economics (55.1), arts (50.7), law and administration (50.3), agriculture (43.8), physical education or sport (37.2), and technical studies (17.4). These ratios have remained largely unchanged since the 1970s.[9]

It is important to note that in Poland there are no university studies related to women's issues (Women's Studies). There are some research centres, lectures, seminars, workshops and conferences, but there is still no opportunity to graduate in the field of women's studies.

There is a fear that the economic transformations and their consequences, such as high unemployment and the difficult living conditions of many households, can act against the education of girls. It continues to be regarded as more economical to invest in the education of a boy, because this gives a better guarantee of finding a job than investing in the long-term education of a girl who is going to become a mother and a housewife anyway.

Employment of Women in Education and Higher Education
Domestic statistics on employment in education are not prepared according to gender; they only reveal that women make up 77 per cent of people employed in this sector. However, personal findings allow us to make the following remarks and conclusions: the percentage of women is highest in primary schools; a man is very often a school principal while the majority of teachers are women;

and more men work in high schools, especially technical schools. More specific data concerning the employment of women in education are available in relation to higher education.

Although women make up the majority of students and graduates, they are less frequently employed as academic assistants, which is the introductory position for an academic career. This is probably a result not so much of discrimination but rather of the unequal participation of women in different departments and of the fact that an application for the position of assistant is a result of a proposal by a tutor, who is usually a man.

The course of the academic career of men and women is different. While in the academic year 1991 women made up 43.1 per cent of assistants, they made up 34.6 per cent of assistant professors, 19.3 per cent of associate professors and 15.1 per cent of professors (see Table 7.2).

Women comprised 29 per cent of those obtaining doctorates in 1985, and 31 per cent in 1990, while those obtaining the degree of doctor habilitated comprised respectively 20 and 21 per cent women. In 1985, fifty-four women were promoted to Associate Professors (18 per cent of the total), while in 1990 seventy-nine women (20 per cent) achieved this rank. In 1985, the title of Professor was given to eighteen women (14 per cent), and in 1990 to thirty-nine women (20 per cent).

Female scientific workers are concentrated in some fields, as can be seen by analysing women's representation among those achieving doctorates and 'doctor habilitated' degrees by separate areas. In 1990, women made up the majority of newly-promoted doctors of pharmacy, almost half of those in biology and medicine, and more than one third of those in law and humanities. Among newly-promoted habilitated doctors, women made up about one third in pharmacy, biology and medicine. In other fields, their participation was smaller (see Table 7.3).

In Poland, there is no wherewithal to support women in attaining higher academic degrees. Family obligations become the reason for the resignation of many women from their academic careers.

TABLE 7.2: Percentage of women among teaching staff in higher education institutions in Poland.

Years	Professors	Associate Professors	Assistant Professors	Assistants
1985–6	12.9	19.4	33.3	38.5
1990–1	15.1	19.3	34.6	43.1

Source: R. Siemienska: 'Academic Careers in Poland: Does Gender Make a Difference?', *Higher Education in Europe,* 17:2 (1992).

TABLE 7.3: 'Doctor habilitated' degrees and doctorates awarded according to scientific field in 1990.

Speciality	Doctor habilitated		Doctor	
	Total	Women	Total	Women
Biology	62	21	164	79
Chemistry	35	5	80	17
Economics	94	26	156	42
Pharmacy	10	4	26	19
Physics	54	4	83	10
Geography	1	–	–	–
Forestry	1	1	5	–
Mathematics	28	4	7	–
Medicine	129	40	455	205
Humanities	187	54	536	192
Political science	1	1	1	–
Technical science	201	7	420	59
Law	38	11	43	16
Agriculture	92	27	173	55
Theology	8	–	25	–
Veterinary	11	1	19	2
Army	12	–	45	–
Physical education	9	–	36	9

Source: R. Siemienska, op. cit., p. 75.

Recommendations

It is necessary to eliminate the texts of manuals which reinforce the stereotypes related to male and female roles. There needs to be a means of supporting women to develop their technical interests and skills. It is desirable to establish undergraduate and graduate programmes of Women's Studies.

Notes

1. Dane GUS, cyt.za *Trybuna Ludu*, no. 227 (29 October 1994).
2. Dane GUS, Aktywnosc zawodowa i bezrobocie w Polsce (Warsaw, November 1994).
3. A. Sucholinska, 'Problem bezrobocia wsrod kobiet', *Wiadomosci Satsytyczne*, 12 (1993).
4. E. Czerwinska, Aktywnosc zawodowa kobiet, Kancelaria Sejmu – Biuro Studiow i Ekspertyz (Warsaw, March 1994).
5. M. Knothe, 'Job Market for Women in Warsaw', *Women and Business*, 2 (1993).
6. A. Rogut, Kobiety w prywatnych przedsiebiorstwach, Instytut Badan nad Demokracja i Przedsiebiorstwem Prywatnym (1994), Warszawa oraz: 'Aktywnosc ekonomiczna ludnosci Polki', *Informacje i opracowania statystyczne* (Warsaw: GUS, 1993).
7. The study was initiated by the International Forum for Women and involved 320 selected women business proprietors in Poland. Ninety-seven responses were received (33 per cent reply rate).
8. I. Nowacka, 'The Image of Women in Schools' Manuals', *Nasza Praca*, The League of Polish Women, no. 6 (1989); and the analysis of current manuals.
9. R. Siemienska, 'Academic Careers in Poland: Does Gender Make a Difference?', *Higher Education in Europe*, 17:2 (1992).

Part 4

Women and Decision-Making, Politics and the Law

Chapter 8

———◆———

DECISION–MAKING, POLITICS AND THE LAW
Kamlesh Bahl

Equality of Opportunity: A Fundamental Aspect of Human Rights

Equal opportunities is important because it is right and fair and just that men and women have equal opportunity. It is a fundamental aspect of human rights. It is also a critical component for business success and the economic prosperity of the UK in an increasingly global and competitive environment. It is about maximising our human resources, women as well as men, to enable businesses and organisations to recover the investments made in every individual and not just a favoured few. It is about allowing each individual to achieve to their full potential. Of course the law itself demands that we treat men and women as individuals, and that they are entitled to equal opportunities as a legal right. In the field of decision-making, there is a fourth very important reason in support of equal representation in the representative and administrative apparatus of nations. Decision-making bodies should be seen to mirror the society that they serve in an effort to ensure that the interests of all are taken into account. The under-representation of women in decision-making prevents full account from being taken of the interests and needs of the population as a whole. This is true of decisions made both by our judges and by our Members of Parliament. However, although women represent more than half of the population of Britain, they continue to be very severely under-represented in all decision-making, whether it is in business or Parliament, and certainly in the legal profession. It is important therefore to consider:

- the current position of women in society, then women in the law and politics;
- the current issues surrounding the position of women in the law and politics;
- suggestions for the way forward.

The Work of the Equal Opportunities Commission

The Commission was set up by Parliament with all-party support in 1975. Although we are funded entirely by government, our statutory role means that we are genuinely independent of government and we can, on occasion, find ourselves challenging government policy. The trick is for us to do this effectively, and at the same time to maintain a good relationship with the government, the Secretary of State for Employment, and the officials of that department. We have up to fifteen Commissioners, all appointed by the Secretary of State for Employment, and there are currently eleven Commissioners representing a broad spectrum of interests.

The Commission has three statutory duties:

- to work towards the elimination of discrimination;
- to promote equality of opportunity between men and women generally;
- to keep under review the working of the Sex Discrimination Act and the Equal Pay Act, and to submit proposals for amending both Acts to the Secretary of State when necessary.

The Commission uses its legal, promotional and research powers strategically and comprehensively to carry out these duties. There are many ways in which these aims can be achieved, but without doubt a strong legal base, both UK and European, has been a significant and unique factor in enabling the Commission to work towards achieving equal opportunities.

The Commission has legal powers, and can:
- assist individuals in taking claims of sex discrimination and equal pay to industrial tribunals;
- take an action of judicial review, to challenge a decision or policy of a public authority: one legal action can change the situation for many, and, if properly targeted, can be more effective than taking an individual case;
- undertake formal investigations. We also have the power to conduct formal investigations based either on a specific belief that an employer is discriminating, or on a more general view of a sector or type of service. These can be very successful in generating changes in attitudes and practices.

The Current Position of Women in Society

Twenty years ago, when the legislation was being discussed in Parliament, there was plenty of evidence that women and men did not have equality of opportunity, and that women suffered systematic discrimination because of their sex. There were, for example, separate wage rates for men and women, often doing the same work side by side. There was a very clear belief that there were 'men's jobs' and 'women's jobs'. A woman could be denied a job just because of her sex. Clearly, we have come a long way since then; but it is important to be aware how much is still to be achieved.

In Scotland today, almost 52 per cent of the population are women, and 48 per cent of all employees are women. Yet twenty years after the Equal Pay Act came into force, women are still paid only 79 per cent of average male earnings. One explanation for this difference is job segregation. Where before the Equal Pay Act there were men's grades and women's grades, now men and women do different jobs. Some 71 per cent of women are employed in a very narrow range of industries, namely public administration, services, distribution, hotels and catering. These jobs, where women are concentrated, have traditionally had a low value, perhaps because they are associated with 'women's work', which runs heavily to skills related to caring and giving service to others. Society had tended to place a very low value on such skills.

Despite the fact that more than 50 per cent of graduates are women and are increasingly better qualified, there are for example only three women directors on the boards of the top twenty Scottish companies. Examing the position of Scottish women, in 1995, we saw that two of the sixty-five Scottish local-authority chief executives were women, yet neither of these women has been appointed to serve in the new local authorities in Scotland which came into existence in April 1996. Indeed, there are no women chief executives in local government in Scotland. At senior levels in industry, in the civil service and in almost every leading profession, women are still scandalously under-represented even though they have been employed in those areas for many years.

The Law
One profession where it is clear that women are under-represented is the law, and in particular women in the judiciary. The Scottish justice system has long been widely admired as a mature and progressive legal order. However, it is also traditionally a world dominated by men, and even the briefest investigation into the position of Scottish women as lawyers reveals that this is slow to change. This is particularly evident in the senior ranks of the profession. Judges and sheriffs are selected from solicitors and advocates, so it is important to look at the numbers of women in these professions. The proportions of women and men on the

solicitors' rolls since 1988, given in Table 8.1, show that in Scotland women solicitors now hold a third of all practising certificates, which compares with 9 per cent twenty years ago.

The proportions of women admitted as solicitors since 1988 are shown in Table 8.2. The position of women solicitors in England and Wales is similar: women hold 27 per cent of practising certificates, compared with 5.2 per cent twenty years ago. The Law Society of England and Wales also analyses the proportion of women solicitors in private practice by position. In 1992, 27.5 per cent of partners were female while 60.8 per cent were male, and 62 per cent of assistant solicitors were female, with men comprising only 22.9 per cent. The Law Society of Scotland does not break down the numbers of practising solicitors in this way, and we would call upon them to do so, for it is only by

TABLE 8.1: Solicitors' rolls.

Year	Women	Men	Total	% Women
1988	2,047	5,976	8,203	25.5
1989	2,235	6,018	8,253	27.1
1990	2,402	6,018	8,510	28.2
1991	2,574	6,166	8,740	29.5
1992	2,780	6,263	9,012	30.8
1993	2,981	6,322	9,303	32
1994	3,136	6,358	9,494	33

Source: The Law Society of Scotland.

TABLE 8.2: Proportions of women admitted as solicitors.

Year	Women	Men	Total	%Women
1988	175	207	382	45.9
1989	214	213	399	48.6
1990	194	205	399	48.6
1991	243	241	484	50.2
1992	205	143	348	58.9
1993	223	201	424	52.6
1994	193	163	356	54.2

Source: The Law Society of Scotland.

monitoring the position that we can obtain a clear picture of the gender balance of the profession. It is clear, however, from anecdotal evidence, that women are highly represented among assistant solicitors, but not among partners, with women taking much longer to achieve a partnership than men. This is true even of those women who have not taken a career break.

The proportion of women practising at the Bar has also increased significantly in recent years, and women now constitute 22 per cent of practising barristers in England and Wales, compared with 7.4 per cent twenty years ago. In Scotland, 64 out of a total of 351 advocates are women, and this represents 18 per cent of all advocates. This increase is not, however, reflected in the proportion of women in the judiciary. In Scotland, the proportion of women sheriffs has hardly altered since 1984, from 5.2 per cent to 7.9 per cent in 1995. There are no women judges (out of twenty-six) in the Court of Session, which is the supreme court in Scotland, and only one temporary judge (out of seven). In England and Wales, the picture is similar, as shown in Table 8.3.

In the UK, the judicial bodies which consider sex-discrimination complaints are the Industrial Tribunals, and we are accordingly particularly interested in the numbers of women represented in these Tribunals. Scotland is very fortunate to have a woman as the President of the Industrial Tribunals. There is however only one full-time female chairman, out of nine, and

TABLE 8.3:   Women in the judiciary in England and Wales.

Position	Number	Percentage
Lords of Appeal in Ordinary	0 (out of 10)	0
Lord Justices of Appeal	1 (out of 29)	3
High Court Judges	6 (out of 95)	6
Circuit Judges	29 (out of 514)	6
Recorders	41 (out of 866)	5
Assistant Recorders	61 (out of 391)	16

Source: Lord Chancellor's Department.

three part-time female chairmen, out of a total of twenty-four. Of the lay members who sit on the industrial tribunals in Scotland, 23 per cent are women. In England and Wales, 11 per cent of full-time chairmen are women, and 7 per cent of part-time chairmen; of the lay members, 28 per cent are women.

Current Issues

The lack of women in the judiciary is a matter in which concern is being expressed both in Scotland and in England and Wales. There was the recent Home Affairs Committee Enquiry into the Appointment Procedures for Judges and Magistrates; and the Lord Chancellor has expressed his concern about the relatively small number of women legal practitioners who seek appointments to judicial office and to Queen's Counsel. Similar concerns have been expressed in Scotland.

It is true that judges and sheriffs are appointed from the senior ranks of the profession, and it has been suggested that because women did not begin to come to the Bar in significant numbers until the late 1970s, there are few women with the requisite experience as yet. This may be part of the reason for women's very slow progress into the ranks of the judiciary, but it is not an unusual explanation in relation to women's participation in other previously male-dominated fields.

It is often said that a greater volume of women entering the profession will mean better representation at higher levels. However, this is not necessarily true. In the teaching profession, which has a high volume of women in the ranks, we have still seen little increase in the number of women at the top: in secondary schools in England and Wales, where nearly half of all teachers are women, women hold only one in five head teachers' posts, while in Scotland the position is much worse, with only fourteen out of 389 head teachers' posts held by women (only 4 per cent).

The law is no different from other professions. We cannot count on mere mass to ensure change at higher levels. What we need is concerted action to dismantle the barriers to the judicial appointments of women; without that, women will continue to be severely under-represented. What then are the barriers?

The Barriers

A major concern for the Commission is the emphasis which continues to be placed in the recruitment procedure on wide confidential consultation with judges and senior practitioners. It is interesting to look at the process of selection of judges and sheriffs in Scotland, who are officially appointed by the Queen. Submissions are made to the Queen by the Secretary of State for Scotland, and nominations to the Secretary of State are made by the Lord Advocate. The Lord Advocate takes advice from a variety of sources, namely the Sheriffs Principal, the Lord President of the Court of Session, the Director of Scottish Courts Administration, the President of the Law Society and the Dean of the Faculty of Advocates, all of whom are currently men.

Given the predominance of men in the senior ranks of the judiciary, the Bar and the solicitors' profession, there is an increased risk of stereotypical assumptions being made with regard to 'female' as opposed to 'male' qualities and aptitudes. There is a tendency to select types with whom the selectors identify, without realising that this might disadvantage women potential candidates. It is therefore the Commission's view that the practice of canvassing opinion is certain to risk introducing impressionistic and subjective factors into the recruitment process. Furthermore, for many reasons (not least family commitments), many women applicants may well not have established an extensive network of professional contacts, thus restricting the spread of senior practitioners and judges who are in a position to comment on them.

Although women constitute 22 per cent of practising barristers, they represent just over 5 per cent of senior counsel. In Scotland, the situation is better, with women constituting 18 per cent of advocates and 8 per cent of Queen's Counsel. Many women barristers are highly critical of the current appointments system for silks, which itself relies heavily upon consultation. Unless more women are appointed as Queen's Counsel, it is unlikely that the number of female High Court judges will increase appreciably in the foreseeable future.

The Way Forward: Transparency, Training and Positive Action
The EOC welcomes the Lord Chancellor's recent initiatives in judicial appointment procedures, particularly open advertisement for appointments, and we would hope to see such initiatives followed in Scotland. This will create the potential to increase the number of women applying for, and appointed to, judicial office. The Lord Chancellor's recent initiatives, however, apply only to those below the level of the High Court. We would urge him to extend these initiatives to all judicial appointments: unless open recruitment is extended at the lower levels, it is unlikely that women will make significant inroads into the senior tiers of the judiciary, as is evidenced by the fact that the number of senior women judges has increased only marginally in the past twenty years. What the EOC wants to see is transparency, training and positive action.

The EOC has recommended that the current system of collecting opinion be replaced by a system which objectively looks at individuals' aptitudes and skills. The current system is subjective and depends on individuals' perceptions of what makes a good member of the judiciary. Qualities such as 'decisiveness' and 'authority' are among the published selection criteria, and judgements on them will be based on an individual's preconceptions. This is a great danger in an area such as the judiciary, which has always been largely male, and seen as a male area of work, so that preconceptions of what makes a good judge are also likely to be male. If the appointments process remains based on such subjective judgements, they will remain a significant barrier to the progress of women.

The EOC has recommended that a programme of positive action be used to encourage sufficient applications from women to ensure that more are encouraged from both branches of the profession to consider applying for judicial office. This is not to say that appointment will be on anything but an equal basis for all individuals. But we must appreciate that, without steps to encourage more applicants, the present situation is most unlikely to change.

Women and Politics

In the political arena, it is clear that women are severely under-represented when the current facts and figures are considered. Participation of women in political life in the UK, although increasing, remains very low:

- the UK currently has sixty women MPs out of 651 (9 per cent)
- only 164 women have been elected to Westminster since 1978
- the UK has a lower percentage of female MPs than any EU country except France and Greece
- out of 1,213 peers, only seventy-nine are women.

In Scotland, the position is similar: only seven out of the seventy-two MPs are women (9 per cent), which is only two more than the number elected in 1959 and 1964.

In local government, the position is not much better. Looking again at Scotland, where local elections took place in April 1995, the situation is as shown in Table 8.4. These elections saw an increase in the proportion of women counsellors of just 0.5 per cent, thus there has been little improvement since the picture in May 1994, as shown in Table 8.5. Looking at the position in the European Parliament, the UK does not compare well with its European counterparts, as shown in Table 8.6.

Current Issues

The Commission has been concerned for many years with the imbalance of women and men in public life and in decision-making generally. With the objective of seeking to achieve equality, it has participated in and led a number of initiatives to increase the representation of women. It is the Commission's view that the decisions taken by individual political parties to achieve a better gender balance are matters for their internal decision-

TABLE 8.4: Local elections, April 1995.

	Women	Men	All	Percentage of women
Labour	145	467	612	24
Conservative	22	60	82	27
Lib Dem	35	88	123	28
SNP	36	145	181	20
Ind./other	21	140	161	15

Source: Scottish Local Government Information Unit.

TABLE 8.5: Local elections, April 1995.

	Women	Men	All	Percentage of women
District Councils	251	907	1,158	22
Regional & Islands Councils	93	441	534	17

Source: Scottish Local Government Information Unit.

TABLE 8.6: Women in the European Parliament, expressed as a percentage.

MEPS	1989	1994
Luxembourg	50	50
Denmark	38	44
Germany	32	34
Spain	15	33
Belgium	17	32
Netherlands	28	32
France	22	30
Ireland	7	27
UK	15	18
Greece	4	16
Italy	12	10
Portugal	13	8
Total	19	25

Source: European Women's Lobby, 1994.

making. These generally fall outside the scope of the Sex Discrimination Act by reason of an exception in the Act. Section 33 of the Act provides exemption for political parties in relation to the provision of services to the public. It is under this section that the policy of the Labour Party of quotas for internal candidates, while clearly a policy of positive discrimination for women, falls. This is a previously untested area of the law, and, when the issue first emerged, the EOC took leading Counsel's opinion on it. We were advised that this policy fell within the exemption in Section 33. We recognise, however, that some lawyers and commentators have expressed a contrary view, and it may well be that the courts will ultimately have to provide an authoritative ruling.

However, consideration must be given to finding ways to encourage participation by currently excluded groups, and in particular to seek to eliminate the barriers to women's participation that have existed in the past. There are no known countries in which women are represented equally with men in the political decision-making processes. In the European Union in 1992, Sweden had the highest participation of women in national government, at 40.4 per cent.[1]

It is widely accepted that women's inequality within the workplace is constructed by the interaction of a number of different factors. Broadly, these are:

- childcare and other domestic responsibilities: unless these can be accommodated, participation by many women is made more difficult;
- lack of education and training opportunities: although on average girls achieve better at school than boys, lower aspirations mean fewer women achieving at higher-education level; employers are considerably less likely to offer training opportunities to women than men;
- traditional attitudes and social pressures: women who do seek to achieve and enter non-traditional occupations often meet opposition and come under pressure from parents, partners and peers; they often find it difficult to fit into a 'male-oriented' culture in the workplace or organisation;
- lack of confidence: many studies have indicated that women generally undervalue their own skills and abilities and are consequently less confident at taking on new tasks, or taking risks in work or political life, than men are;
- low wages or dependence on benefits: women earn substantially less than men, are often economically dependent on a man and are more likely to be dependent on state benefits. They therefore often do not have transport or financial resources, such as money to pay babysitters, that would enable them to participate in external activities.

For black and ethnic-minority women, these barriers are further compounded by double discrimination arising from different language, and also by the impact of racial discrimination and prejudice. For example, ethnic-minority women's unemployment rate, at 16 per cent, is far higher than white women's, which is 6 per cent. Yet because they are, on average, younger than white women, more will be entering the labour market, and they are more likely to continue education after school. They experience worse terms and conditions of employment, including rates of pay.

The Way Forward
In politics, the barriers for women have been found to come together into an underlying alienation of women from legislative institutions. Consideration must therefore be given to ways of removing the social and economic barriers to women in political participation. For example:

Positive Action measures to attract women and other under-represented groups into the formal political process should be considered. It is important to undertake a programme of awareness-raising, training and confidence-building to encourage women to put themselves forward for election and to ensure that those who do come forward have the necessary skills.

Transparency in recruitment procedures: positive action strategies are a matter for the parties themselves, but care should be taken to ensure that the procedures themselves do not disadvantage women candidates. The Commission advises that selection procedures should be transparent, open and accessible.

Finally, consideration must be given to ways in which the structural and situational barriers to women's participation in political life can be removed. For example, membership of councils and public appointments will need to be adequately waged, and should not be a voluntary activity, and the hours and times of working will require to be changed, and there needs to be support to meet childcare and other caring needs.

Note
1. Engender Audit (1995).

Chapter 9

◆

PRACTICAL SKILLS FOR THE POLITICAL ARENA

Lesley Abdela

Why the World Needs Parity Democracy

Women having a proper say at all the decision-making levels of society is absolutely central to the development of both the urban economy and the political life of a modern democracy. The world is in a terrible mess: massive unemployment across Western, Central and Eastern Europe; over thirty wars waging, including one in the heart of Europe; tremendous damage to our environment; a worse global imbalance of rich and poor than ever before; racism, ethnic hatreds and anti-Semitism resurging across Europe; millions starving around the world; and the problems of migrations of millions of people.

Even beyond fair play for the majority gender, if we are to have a chance of solving these massive problems facing us on this planet, our leaders need to be chosen from the widest available pool of talent, without narrowing the choice to half the pool. Women are dramatically under-represented in parliaments and governments. Top positions in politics, banks, international organisations such as the European Commission, the UN, NATO, the World Bank and other powerful groups are predominantly held by men. Thus men set the priorities for the allocation of finances, welfare services, education, trade, agriculture, international relations, health services etc.

On the international scale, very often it is women – by the million – who suffer the most serious consequences of very bad decisions made by politicians; in former Yugoslavia, 80 per cent of refugees and displaced people are women. But does it matter whether there are 300 women or no women in Parliament? The answer is a definite yes. It is not possible or desirable to depute so overwhelmingly another gender to express the needs and wishes of women. A gender imbalance in any parliament means that the majority gender's needs get grotesquely overlooked. Research in the USA shows that elected women of any political party are 50 per cent more likely to take up issues of concern to women than elected men.

Throughout the twentieth century, government after government has tended to ignore, even to disdain, what women want and need. In every country, there is a long list of policies which overlook or damage women. Just a few examples are that most women are paid less than men for work of similar value; in too many countries, domestic violence against women and sexual harassment are considered 'normal', millions of women are in low-paid, low-status work; and lack of affordable, good-quality childcare is often a major block for women needing to earn their living.

The twentieth century's experience shows that until women, as women, achieve numbers in the legislatures far nearer parity, all advances in politics, public life and the passing of legislation of especial importance to the majority gender should be viewed as extremely fragile and easily reversible.

Change the Political Culture: 'Shevolution'

The aim of the game is to reach full 'shevolution' – a word I invented to describe what happens when the proper balance of women's and men's talents operates in a culture that suits both genders comfortably. It is important to urge more women to put themselves forward in politics and public life, but at the same time national and international organisations must change their existing power structures to accommodate women equally with men. One way to accomplish this vital aim would be to encourage the formation of indigenous '300 GROUPS' in the new nations of Central and Eastern Europe, such as the new '222 Group' in Romania. From the hundreds of discussions that I have had in the past few years with women in other countries, I am convinced that the 300 GROUP system which we have used in the UK could be invaluable, adapted to other cultures.

Many people think that the UK has been a democratic country for at least 300 years, ruled wisely by the 'Mother of Parliaments'. In fact, nothing like true democracy existed here until after the 1914–18 War, when in late 1918 women over 30 years of age won the right to vote and to stand for Parliament. Yet three generations later, in 1979, when Margaret Thatcher was elected as Britain's first woman prime minister, she was one of only nineteen women out of 635 Members of Parliament. The number of women MPs had even declined over the previous decade.

Why So Few Women MPs?
There were serious reasons why so few women were standing for Parliament. First, there was a long-standing belief by women and men that politics was a 'man's game' and that women candidates would be an electoral liability. This manifested itself in unsubstantiated prejudices by members of Party Committees involved in selecting candidates. 'She's too pretty', 'she's too old', 'she should stay home and look after her children/does your husband know you're here?', 'her heels are too high', 'she wears too many rings on her fingers', 'factory workers don't vote for a woman', 'fishermen/farmers won't vote for a woman'.

This was all proved to be utterly untrue. Research shows that voters do not discriminate against women parliamentary candidates. In fact, in some instances, women do slightly better than men in similar constituencies. This is re-emphasised by the high proportion of women in the past fifteen years who have won seats in by-elections. In a by-election (often caused by the death of the incumbent), the performance of the individual candidate comes under much more scrutiny than in a general election, yet women candidates in all the major parties have won by-elections by record percentages throughout the 1980s and 1990s.

Second, until the 1980s, there was a complete lack of interest by the political parties in encouraging women to stand for elected office, except at the Town Hall level. Third, no organisation existed which was specifically designed to inform women about the influence of Parliament on their everyday lives and how they themselves could become very well-qualified parliamentary candidates.

Action for Change in the UK: The 300 GROUP

In 1980, we formed that missing organisation. We called it the 300 GROUP, the target being at least 300 women MPs. The 300 GROUP is an all-party group which aims to get many more women elected to local councils and Parliament. The 300 GROUP is a system that can transfer to any other country, and is a training, advice and encouragement organisation, with a committed campaigning style. The 300 GROUP trains many more women to enter the political arena and at the same time campaigns to change the culture in the political and press and media arena to make it more welcoming to women.

As well as training and encouraging hundreds of women to stand for local, national and European elected office, a number of important spin-off developments have occurred directly and indirectly as a result of actions by the original 300 GROUP. When the 300 GROUP started, there was virtually no coverage of the issue of women in politics in the British press and media; now there are frequent features and programmes. In 1980, the political parties were, at best, indifferent to the lack of women Members of Parliament; now they compete to find ways of increasing the number of women candidates.

Women in UK Politics Today

Fourteen years since the 300 GROUP started, the situation for women in politics in the UK is optimistic. Within three general elections, we have gone from nineteen to sixty-two women in the House of Commons, more women MPs than ever before in our history. The doors are opening for women to have a greater say in running the country and the European Union at all levels than ever before. The press and media have become more and more interested in the topic, and many more women are stepping forward into local, national and European politics. The Speaker and Deputy Speaker of the House of Commons are both women: Betty Boothroyd and Janet Fookes. Although sixty-two women MPs out of 651 is just under 10 per cent, it does mean that there are now women highly visible in the 'corridors of power' and on the important committees in Parliament, as well as visible and audible in the Chamber and available through the media. Issues of importance to women are moving higher up the political agenda with every passing year and every general election.

Equalising Action

It is not enough to urge more women to stand for office without looking at the practical problems that need to be removed. I believe that it may be important to look at the quota system or other equalising structures with new eyes. In practically every political system, there is open and hidden positive discrimination in favour of men. To counterbalance these unfair advantages, left-of-centre parties in Norway, Sweden, Germany and the UK have introduced equalising action quota rules to increase the number of women parliamentary candidates. These systems have worked successfully.

- Following the 1995 Swedish election, nearly 41 per cent of the elected MPs were women and half the government ministers were women.
- 41 per cent of the Norwegian Parliament are women, as are nearly half the cabinet ministers, including the prime minister, Gro Harlem Brundtland.
- 33 per cent of the Danish Parliament are women.
- 21 per cent of the German Members of Parliament are women.

In the UK, the highest increase in women candidates has been made in the left-of-centre parties, which have introduced equalising action rules. In the Liberal Democrat Party, at least one third of each constituency shortlist of parliamentary candidates has to be women, and one third men. In the Labour Party, 50 per cent of all target winnable seats in the party will be reserved for women-only shortlists of candidates, though admittedly this has run to open controversy.

The Gender Gap

Women's campaigning groups in the USA and the UK are using the Gender Gap in voting to point out to male politicians that they need to respond to what women voters want. In the USA, women voters have been the deciding factor in putting over 134 senators in or out of office, and in throwing George Bush out of the Presidency. Since 1987, there have been more women than men voters in the UK. The Gender Gap has appeared in the UK as it has in the USA. Groups of women are voting en bloc differently from equivalent groups of men. For example, women under 30 years of age are less likely to support the Conservative Party than men in the same age group. Politicians are slowly realising that they will need to pay more attention to what women want.

In the UK, we used the seventy-fifth anniversary of women's suffrage as an occasion to hold the first House of Commons 'Week of Women'. Over seventy speakers – women and men experts working in the 'front line' with battered women, carers, pensioners, women in business, training, lone parents, rural women, urban women – outlined what policies are urgently needed. From those talks, I compiled a guidebook entitled *What Women Want* for politicians and policymakers.[1] The book is sponsored by The Body Shop Foundation, and a copy was mailed to every elected Member of Parliament and to editors and journalists.

The Way Forward: Causing Change

Democracy cannot be called true democracy when over half the population are not properly represented at all decision-making levels. This is not a question of the exclusion of men from the political process; rather, it is the question of the *inclusion* of women.

Change happens in a democracy when enough people want that change to happen. Over the past decade, the issue of increasing the number of women at all levels of politics in Western European and North American democracies has been a slow but steady success story. Advances have been made because of hard work and determined campaigning combined with sheer practical advice, training, support and information for women prepared to enter public and political life by groups like the independent, all-party 300 GROUP for Women In Politics/Public Life in the UK, and by groups of women within the political parties campaigning for change. These multiple approaches will also be crucial if women in Central and Eastern Europe are to gain a powerful say in the future of their countries.

Note

1. L. Abdela (comp.), *What Women Want: A Guide to Creating a Better and Fairer Life for Women in the UK*, in association with the Body Shop (The Body Shop International, 1994).

Part 5

International Networking

---◆---

Chapter 10

Setting up the European Women's Lobby

Lesley Sutherland

The Establishment of the European Women's Lobby

In 1987 a conference was held, attended by non-governmental organisations from across Europe, at which the need for a European women's network was discussed. Given the increasing impact of European legislation and case law, and the sharing of experience that had already taken place, there was a clear consensus that such a network was required in order to ensure that women's concerns, priorities and agendas were delivered at a European level. I first became involved at a conference held in Scotland in October 1988, to discuss the Scottish perspective of the project. This coincided with the revitalisation of the debate on the governance of Scotland and the renewed demand for some form of Scottish Parliament. Among women activists, there was also the conviction that if the shortcomings of democracy in Scotland were to be tackled, then no longer would the marginalisation of half the population, namely women, be accepted; any campaign to expand democracy would have to include ensuring women's equal status and participation. Consequently, there was agreement from that conference that there should indeed be a European body; furthermore, there should be direct Scottish input. In this matter we were supported, in particular, by our sisters in Northern Ireland, reflecting both a concern that the representation from the UK should not be delivered solely through a perspective from the south-east, and the different legal systems, education systems and languages which exist within the UK. We were successful in convincing our English sisters, and fortunately four seats per member state were allocated at the Lobby, allowing one seat for each part of the UK.

With the support of pre-existing organisations, we therefore set about establishing four new networks in the UK – a task not without its problems. However, when the Lobby held its General Assembly, the four representatives were there from the UK, working together. Although each of the organisations is autonomous, we coordinate our efforts through a joint committee and agree, for example, who will be the Board member from the UK. I have represented the Women's Forum Scotland since 1990 at the General Assembly and have also been the UK Board member since then, and am currently the Treasurer of the Lobby. I hope to be re-elected for 1996 to serve out my term as Treasurer, after which I will be no longer eligible for the Board.

The Lobby itself is composed of representatives of women's non-governmental organisations from the member states and of European women's NGOs or women's sections of mixed NGOs. Member states have discretion as to how they arrange their representation, provided that it complies with the Statutes. Therefore, Ireland's four representatives come from one organisation, as do Germany's, while Belgium is represented through two organisations. Examples of European organisations include business and professional women, women in medicine, law or agricultural professions, university women, black women in the arts, European Trade Union Confederation, Jewish women, Catholic women, and so on.

One of the prerequisites of a successful network was therefore met; there was a need, widely recognised, for such a structure. Consensus was also achieved on the objectives, composition and membership requirements of the Lobby. There had been some discussion about whether political parties could affiliate, but this was rejected as it was deemed crucial that the Lobby should be seen to be acting independently of political parties and could therefore more readily lobby them. Conversely, some argued that there was no need for the Lobby, as women could be represented through the existing structures of, for example, the European Parliament and by women Parliamentarians. This ignored the under-representation of women in political parties, Parliament and other decision-making structures, and the difficulties which women experience in having their concerns recognised and addressed in a way they find acceptable. Having agreed these basic principles and set itself up, the Lobby then had to meet another challenge to becoming a successful network, namely resources, or, more bluntly, money. The Lobby receives an annual subvention from the European Union. Although it might seem strange that the institutions which the Lobby seeks to influence enable it to do so, it is consistent with the European Union's view on the expression of legitimate interest groups. However, the Lobby has not only to make application each year for funding but also to lobby for it and for any increase in it. This year, the Lobby receives 450,000 Ecus in subvention. While that might seem a large amount, in reality it is very little. Although women are half the population, and through our member organisations the Lobby covers some 2,500 organisations, the subvention received is very low down the list of those which receive money from the same budget line.

For women's networks, this aspect is crucial, as very often women's organisations themselves are underfunded. A small and very dedicated staff is employed in Brussels. Participation in the Lobby has made clear the difference in relationship between women's NGOs and their governments in the different European countries. Some are accorded substantial subventions and are regularly consulted, while others receive nothing and are almost disregarded. Recognising this, the Lobby fully funds attendance at its General Assembly, held annually, as otherwise some countries would be unrepresented. As this is the only occasion on which all delegates have a chance to meet and, indeed, network, this expense is justified. Another item of expenditure is interpreting at the Assembly. Although many from the smaller countries do speak more than one language, it is also felt to be important to allow everyone to speak in the language of their own country, although interpreting is into English, French, German and Spanish. This year, the senior interpreter asked me to intervene to ask delegates to speak their own language and not English, for example, as those interpreting Dutch, Greek and Danish were under-used. Also, as a Scottish Treasurer, I felt it imperative that, having hired one of the few Finnish interpreters available, full use should be made of the facility. The topic of language is further discussed below.

Overcoming Initial Problems

The Lobby is more than one network, through which members have access to other networks. An indication of the range of membership is given above, and recently the Lobby obtained funding to compile a membership directory which comprises not only Lobby members' addresses but also those of its members' members – some 2,500 in all – plus other helpful information.

Having identified the need, identified potential participants, established criteria, set up the organisation and obtained some resources, the next challenge to be addressed was to justify the Lobby and establish its credibility. While I believe that this has been done, it has not always been a smooth path, and certainly not as easy as might originally have been thought. At the first Board meeting after the Lobby had been founded, twenty women came together from across Europe to play their part in taking the organisation forwards. All were committed to the principle of equality and recognised that Europe had a sufficient impact, for good or ill, on women's lives. What, however, were we to do now? So much energy and enthusiasm had been directed towards the establishment of the Lobby that very little had been done in terms of thinking about how it went about its business thereafter. No censure is intended of those who had expended so much time, effort and commitment in creating the Lobby, but it is one of the lessons that I have learnt about setting up a network of this kind in terms of first priorities.

First of all, there were language problems. It had been agreed that Board meetings would be conducted in English and French. What rapidly became apparent was that although most had a fair facility with one of those, not everyone could readily understand or communicate in both. Some members argued that this should be the case, that is, that members should only nominate those with fluency in both languages. I have consistently opposed this position, as it confines members' freedom to nominate those whom they think best suited to meet their criteria; many women are not afforded the opportunity to study languages, and for non-francophone or non-anglophone countries it would mean knowing two additional languages. More importantly, whether or not it should be the case, it patently was not, and so something had to be done to address the issue. In the beginning, we interpreted among ourselves. This left those of us who undertook this task utterly drained, combined as it was with the effort of making an individual contribution. Subsequently, the Lobby has engaged an interpreter who does consecutive interpreting at Board meetings, which, although time-consuming, nevertheless ensures that everyone understands and can contribute.

But the language problems were not just linguistic problems. While we used similar terminologies of equality and inclusion and of lobbying and influencing, it became clear that we did not always mean or understand the same things by those terms. Different histories in different countries, different starting points and different socio-political climates all contributed to different perspectives as to the appropriate matters to be taken up and how that should be done. In the case of several member states, it is less than twenty-five years since they gained freedom from fascist dictatorships or military junta, which presented hugely different challenges to the women's and equality movements compared to elsewhere in Europe at that time. Unsurprisingly, there were many committed Europeans, in the sense of supporting and promoting closer union and convergence. They found it hard to understand those who took a more agnostic approach of 'since we're in, we'd better get involved and see how it goes', and particularly difficult to comprehend those who were distinctly unsure about Europe. Differences in approach, whether more structured or spontaneous, also emerged. The appointment of the General Secretary was a case in point. It took a long time to reach consensus on how this should be done. Finally, it was done with an outcome that everyone could endorse and feel comfortable with, but that took time and negotiation and listening and reviewing. There was less divergence over the Lobby's priorities, but even so, a basic modus operandi had to be talked through. This process was crucial to the sound foundation of the Lobby. The key lesson which I drew from this is that it is not enough to use the same words, and it is rash to assume understanding in this international context without working it through.

The Work of the European Women's Lobby

The Lobby has worked on a number of issues, including women and decision-making, with a particular focus on the European elections of 1994, violence, and black and migrant women, as well as monitoring European policy and instruments and trying to influence them. Recognising that while women are marginalised in European society, some women are even further marginalised, the Lobby commissioned a report, written by black and migrant women, some of whom expressed critical views. For some members of the Lobby, this was an uncomfortable experience, yet the value of this initiative was confirmed when the European Parliament agreed to publish the report, which has now been launched. This activity has put the Lobby in contact with a range of organisations and has contributed a space for some women to express their views to a much wider network. In a similar vein the Lobby, is in contact with women's organisations in Central and Eastern Europe and exchanges information and experience in setting up networks and of the operation of the European Union. This is particularly important for those countries which may be applying for membership.

Much of the agenda of the Lobby naturally follows the agenda of the European Union. Our member-state representatives can be helpful in linking up with the government that holds the presidency, which is very important when this changes every six months and priorities and emphases can change accordingly. On such issues as the maternity directive, one of our early activities, we worked closely with one of the networks to which I am linked: the trades unions. The Lobby has been following and contributing to discussions on the Fourth Action Programme on Equal Opportunities, which will run from 1996 to 2000, providing another example of interlinking networks, as Women's Forum Scotland has been one of the main organisations working with the Equal Opportunities Commission in Scotland on this self-same topic. The theme of women and decision-making which was part of the Third Action Programme is expected to be further developed in the Fourth, as the discussion papers deal with different forms of citizenship and participation. This is an area where women activists in Scotland have very relevant experience through their discussions and campaigning on gender equality and the shape and operating procedures of a future Scottish Parliament. The values of intersecting networks to exchange and interact in relation to these different levels of decision-making and activity becomes ever more apparent.

This leads on to one of the priorities of the Lobby currently. The Lobby has obtained funding for a project on Women and the Construction of Europe, the aim of which is to develop strategies and proposals as to how Europe can become a fairer and more equal place for us all who live there, both male and female. A network of experts, one per member state, has been appointed to draft proposals and make recommendations to the Lobby. One obvious issue which has to be addressed is the framework which underpins the European Union, that is, the treaties. This is all the more pertinent in that the treaties are to come under consideration at the Inter-Governmental Conference (IGC) due to take place under the Irish Presidency in late 1996. Among the initial recommendations made by the expert group, taken on board at the Lobby's recent General Assembly, is that equality should become a cornerstone of the Union in the same way as principles such as 'subsidiarity' are, and should be integrated into the founding articles of the Treaty. The role of the NGOs should be recognised and consideration should be given to according NGOs the status of social partners. Much work remains to be done on elaborating these ideas. Again, however, the process is significantly important; the member organisations will be consulted on their views and hear those from elsewhere. It is expected that while there will be consensus overall, not all member organisations will have the same view. For example, while the UK members generally prefer the move to qualified majority voting as a means for minimising the possibility for one country to block initiative by wielding the absolute veto, the Finnish delegates were concerned that it might reduce the decision-making powers of the smaller countries. The project overall will enable the Lobby to stimulate dialogue within and among its members, and will both inform them about Europe and also stimulate further activity on equality in decision-making, participation and democracy at local and national levels.

The Lobby has played a key role in the preparations for the United Nations Conference on Women in Beijing in September 1995. Both in developing positions and in acting as a clearing house for information and ideas, the Lobby has had a high profile. From my own direct experience of attending a UN Conference for the first time in Copenhagen this year (the Social Summit), I know how important it is to 'hit the ground running' and to be able to lock into what is happening, to know which are the important sessions to hear, caucuses to attend and briefings to obtain, in order both to understand and report back as well as to ensure that the input which we want to make has an impact. For women, this is all the more important and usually all the more difficult. Even although Beijing is the 'women's summit', this knowledge will be crucial. Although we in the northern hemisphere and in Western Europe must acknowledge that the problems of inequality confronted by our sisters elsewhere in the world are frequently of a different magnitude, it is still important that a European perspective be delivered at such conferences. There are significant and relevant experiences that we have to relate and share, and these are of both success and failure. As Peter Townsend, a well-known British social scientist, commented at a meeting in Copenhagen, while in Europe there is wealth there is also growing poverty and inequality, so that Europe is far from having the solutions. Therefore, it is far from a complacent perspective that the European view should be delivered. Again, this affords the opportunity of an example of interleaving networks. Europe has much to learn from elsewhere; and indeed an organisation in Edinburgh, a member and supporter of Women's Forum Scotland, facilitates just such exchanges of information. Scottish Education for Action and Development (SEAD) works at the local community level, linking Scotland with the developing countries.

I have tried to identify some of the key features of networks of the more formal kind at an international level: identification of purpose and goals, meeting a need or closing a gap, consensus and support, resources, achieving a common language and understanding, agreeing on agenda and methodology, gaining credibility and recognition. Resources cannot be underestimated in their importance, and regrettably all too often women have to make do. One of the crucial features of networks which work is the information flow, and here there is unfortunately a shortfall. Because of the commitments to participation referred to above, the Lobby has little money to communicate the very high quality of information which it generates, and that is often compounded by a similar lack of resources further down the chain, for example in the UK. That is a battle to be continued; and perhaps even more vital is the need to establish a common language. Having had the experience described above where women talking about 'equality' had to work hard to establish common understanding, how much more important it then is that with men the same task is undertaken. There has been work done recently on the different 'languages' that women and men speak, leading to misunderstanding and frustration. In my view, it should not simply be women learning to speak the 'other' language, and therefore all the responsibility lying always with them to smooth the path to understanding, but perhaps everyone learning a new vocabulary and syntax. And, if this is to be truly inclusive, we need to look at young and old, and the interconnections between all different networks and layers. To tell, recount experience, interpret, create understanding, persuade and convince requires a common language and meaning. Undertaking that work and disseminating and communicating it is one of the key roles of networks.

NOTES ON CONTRIBUTORS

Lesley Abdela

Lesley Abdela is the senior partner in Eyecatcher Consultants, Conock Manor, Wiltshire. She is a journalist and broadcaster, writing features in *The Times, The Guardian*, the *Financial Times, The Independent, Reader's Digest* etc. She is a frequent speaker at national and international conferences, conducts training and advises employers on women's development issues. She was the political editor for the UK's best-selling women's monthly magazine, *Cosmopolitan.*

Lesley Abdela is the UK consultant on 'Women and Democracy' for Harvard University's 'Project Liberty', organising and conducting workshops with women politicians, campaigners, NGO leaders and the press and media in Poland, the Czech Republic, Slovakia, Hungary, Romania and Bulgaria. In the UK, Lesley Abdela founded the all-party 300 GROUP campaign, which trains women for public and political life. The 300 GROUP campaigns to get more women elected to Parliament, local councils and the European Parliament. She has herself been a parliamentary candidate in the UK. She was a trainer for the United Nations/British Council on the 'Beijing Express', a train travelling in late August 1995 from Warsaw to Beijing for the UN Fourth World Conference on Women, with 300 Central European women aboard.

Kamlesh Bahl

Kamlesh Bahl was appointed Chairwoman of the Equal Opportunities Commission in June 1993. She is a solicitor with a background in commercial law and strategic management, and currently also works as a legal consultant with Data Logic Ltd. Kamlesh obtained her Ll.B. Honours from Birmingham University and then served articles with the Greater London Council from 1978–80. Employed as a legal adviser for Texaco Ltd from 1984–7, Kamlesh was involved in developing and implementing equal-opportunities policies, and from 1981–4 she specialised in employment and health and safety matters at British Steel Corporation.

Kamlesh has been a Council Member of the Law Society since 1990 and is a former Chairman of their Commerce and Industry Group. She was a member of the Ethnic Minorities Advisory Committee of the Lord Chancellor's Judicial Studies Board in 1991 and was a member of the UK delegation to the Fourth World Conference on Women in Beijing in September 1995.

Among her many appointments, Kamlesh is a member of the Council of the National Association of Health Authorities and Trusts and an independent member of the Diplomatic Service Appeal Board of the Foreign and Commonwealth Office. She is also the European Commission's representative on the European Council's Consultative Commission on Racism and Xenophobia, and is a Patron of the 1995 United Nations' Year of Tolerance.

Sheena Briley

Sheena Briley is the director of TRAINING 2000, the charity working to promote women's training and development. TRAINING 2000 is a membership organisation, offering a wide range of services including an extensive events programme, research and consultancy, publications, a quarterly magazine and an information service.

Sheena Briley has extensive experience of working on women's training and development issues. She is the co-author of *Developing Women Managers: Current Issues and Good Practice* (1994), and was Seminar Director for the British Council's International Seminar, 'Women in the Workforce: Human Resource Development Strategies into the Next Century', on which this book is based. She is currently involved in a project exploring equality issues for female students from Scotland and the Ukraine, and is producing a documentary film on this for television.

Lex Gold

Lex Gold is Director of the Scottish Chambers of Commerce. The major part of his career has been spent in the Civil Service. He started in the Inland Revenue and served for twenty-five years in the Home Office in a variety of areas including the Immigration Establishment Police and Prison Departments. He was a 'sherpa' at the G7 summit in Ottawa. During his time in the Home Office, he helped to provide policy advice to a range of other countries and spent four years on secondment with the Civil Service Department.

In 1987, Lex came back to Scotland to take up the post of Manpower Services Commission Director for Scotland. He helped to lead the Preparations for the introduction of Scottish Enterprise and became its first employee in October 1990, when he took up the post of Managing Director, Corporate Services. He helped to establish the new networked organisation. He set up Scotland Europa and became its first Chairman. His thirty-three years in public service ended in March 1993, when his Managing Director's post disappeared on reorganisation. Lex took early retirement. After a short sabbatical, he helped to set up a joint venture for British Polythene PLC in Guandong Province, China. He then served as CB! Director Scotland for just under two years. He took up his present post as Director of the Scottish Chambers of Commerce at the beginning of January 1996.

Christina Hartshorn

Christina Hartshorn is the founding director of the Women's Enterprise Unit, Scottish Enterprise Foundation. Her early career was in careers guidance, specialising in advising women wanting to return to the workforce. In 1987, she was awarded the UK Equal Opportunity Fellowship of the German Marshall Foundation to review business support provision for women in the USA.

She developed and directed Scotland's first business start-up programmes for women, and created the 'Women's Enterprise Roadshow', Scotland's own enterprise awareness campaign. With her colleague Pat Richardson, she was commissioned by the Department of Employment to write the UK guidelines to policy and best practice for women in starting a business. She has extensive experience of working with women business owners in Europe and Asia in both developed and developing economies. She is currently directing a programme of business start-up training for women in Bombay, funded by the Overseas Development Administration. She is also advising governments and non-governmental organisations to plan careers guidance centres for women in southern India and Sri Lanka.

Marilyn McDougall

Marilyn McDougall is a Senior Lecturer in the Department of Management at Glasgow Caledonian University. She has worked in industry in senior Human Resource Management positions in a number of organisations, including Procter and Gamble Ltd and

Playtex Ltd, and she is currently actively involved in management training and consultancy with a range of private, public and voluntary sector organisations.

Marilyn's academic subject is Human Resource Development, which she teaches on postgraduate Diploma and Masters programmes, and on which she has published two books and various journal articles. She is particularly interested in gender issues in career development, especially the progress of women in management. In 1990, she managed the first research project in Scotland on identifying women's management training needs, and she is the co-author with Sheena Briley of *Developing Women Managers: Current Issues and Good Practice* (1994). Her other research interests include peer mentoring and career management. She is married, has two children and lives in Glasgow.

Angela O'Hagan

Angela O'Hagan is Development Officer with the Equal Opportunities Commission for Scotland. She has a background in local government economic development and industrial promotion, specialising in support to small businesses. She was a business adviser to the arts, in a partnership project with Edinburgh District Council and Workshop and Artists' Studio Provision Scotland Ltd.

Linking skills development with organisational effectiveness and economic development, Angela has experience as a freelance consultant and trainer, working with a range of LEC-based contracts across occupational sectors, delivering trainer and assessor training and assessment to TDBL standards as part of NETT strategies throughout the LEC network in Scotland. Part of the consultancy work included developing competence frameworks for economic development practitioners and small-business support programmes.

As an equal-opportunities trainer, Angela has worked with a range of organisations, and prior to joining the Equal Opportunities Commission in November 1993 she led the Arts Management Initiative Training Programme in Scotland on equal opportunities.

Lesley Sutherland

Lesley Sutherland graduated M.A. Honours in French and Drama in 1973, and Master of Education in 1978, and achieved her teaching certificate in 1975. In 1992, she graduated, again from the University of Glasgow, M.Phil. in Industrial Relations, undertaken through part-time study. She has worked as Research Officer for the National Unions of Students Scotland and then Education Officer in the Scottish Vocational Education Council, before taking up her current post as Education and Research Officer for the Transport and General Workers Union.

Lesley has a long-standing commitment to and record of activity in equal opportunities. Elected to represent Women's Forum Scotland at the European Women's Lobby since its establishment in 1990, she has played a key role in the Lobby's development as UK member of its Board and now as Treasurer. Lesley has participated in a number of international conferences, and her particular interests include women and decision-making, participation in representative structures, and education and training; she has been closely involved in TRAINING 2000 from its inception, and is currently Treasurer and Vice-Chair.

Particular thanks are also due to the following contributors. **Dr Nomcebo O. Simelane** and **Nonhlanhla F. Dlamini** of the University of Swaziland, the International Planned Parenthood Federation, Africa Region, and **Mrs M. Khoza**, Principal of the Swaziland Institute of Management and Public Administration, kindly allowed an extract from their 1995 study 'Legal and Policy Barriers Affecting Delivery of Family Planning Services in Swaziland' to be included in this publication.

From the Polish Committee of NGOs, **Maria Anna Knothe** of the Centre for the Advancement of Women, and **Ewa Lizowska** and **Elzbieta Wlodyka** of the International Forum for Women, and **Elzbieta Kalinowska**, kindly allowed the inclusion in this publication of an extract from their report made to the United Nations Fourth World Conference on Women, Beijing, China, September 1995.

INDEX

HMSO Bookshops
71 Lothian Road, Edinburgh EH3 9AZ
0131-479 3141 Fax 0131-479 3142
49 High Holborn, London WC1V 6HB
(counter service only)
0171-873 0011 Fax 0171-831 1326
68-69 Bull Street, Birmingham B4 6AD
0121-236 9696 Fax 0121-236 9699
33 Wine Street, Bristol BS1 2BQ
0117 9264306 Fax 0117 9294515
9-21 Princess Street, Manchester M60 8AS
0161-834 7201 Fax 0161-833 0634
16 Arthur Street, Belfast BT1 4GD
01232 238451 Fax 01232 235401
The HMSO Oriel Bookshop
The Friary, Cardiff CF1 4AA
01222 395548 Fax 01222 384347

Published by HMSO and available from:

HMSO Publications Centre
(Mail, fax and telephone orders only)
PO Box 276, London SW8 5DT
Telephone orders 0171-873 9090
General enquiries 0171-873 0011
(queuing system in operation for both numbers)
Fax orders 0171-873 8200

HMSO's Accredited Agents
(see Yellow Pages)

and through good booksellers